T0163207

LAKE DISTRICT
LOW LEVEL
AND LAKE WALKS

by Vivienne Crow

JUNIPER HOUSE, MURLEY MOSS,
OXENHOLME ROAD, KENDAL, CUMBRIA LA9 7RL
www.cicerone.co.uk

© Vivienne Crow 2014
First edition 2014
ISBN: 978 1 85284 734 0
Reprinted 2017, 2018 and 2020 (with updates)

Printed in China on responsibly sourced paper on behalf of Latitude Press Ltd
A catalogue record for this book is available from the British Library.
All photographs are by the author unless otherwise stated.

Acknowledgements

As a Lake District addict, I am always grateful to the many organisations – often dependant on the work of volunteers – that help make walking in the National Park as safe and as enjoyable as possible. These include the National Trust, the Lake District National Park Authority, the Friends of the Lake District, Fix the Fells, various local authorities and, of course, the hard-working Mountain Rescue teams.

Also, I'd like to thank Heleyne and Jess for being such good company on many of the walks in this book.

Updates to this Guide

While every effort is made by our authors to ensure the accuracy of guidebooks as they go to print, changes can occur during the lifetime of an edition. Any updates that we know of for this guide will be on the Cicerone website (www.cicerone.co.uk/734/updates), so please check before planning your trip. We also advise that you check information about such things as transport, accommodation and shops locally. Even rights of way can be altered over time. We are always grateful for information about any discrepancies between a guidebook and the facts on the ground, sent by email to updates@cicerone.co.uk or by post to Cicerone, Juniper House, Murley Moss, Oxenholme Road, Kendal LA9 7RL.

Register your book: To sign up to receive free updates, special offers and GPX files where available, register your book at www.cicerone.co.uk.

Front cover: On the delightful valley path below High Rigg (Walk 23)
Facing page: Bow Fell towering over upper Eskdale (Walk 16)

CONTENTS

Buttermere (Walk 18)

Route symbols on OS map extracts
(for OS legend see printed OS maps)

N

∼   route   🚶 (⊕) start/finish point

∼   alternative/link   🚶 (⊕) start point
     route

◀   direction of walk   🚶 (⊕) finish point

0   ½ mile

0   1km
        1:40,000

Distance	Grade	Time	Page
10.3km (6½ miles)	2	3½hrs	**22**
11.3km (7 miles)	1/2	3hrs	**28**
7.6km (4¾ miles)	2	2¾hrs	**34**
16.7km (10.4 miles)	3	5¼hrs	**38**
6.5km (4 miles)	2	2¼hrs	**44**
9.8km (6 miles)	3/4	3½hrs	**49**
11.4km (7 miles)	2	3¼hrs	**54**
15.6km (9¾ miles)	2/3	4½hrs	**59**
11km (7 miles)	2	3¼hrs	**67**
12.9km (8 miles)	4	4hrs	**72**
9.4km (6 miles)	1	2½hrs	**78**
11km (7 miles)	5	4hrs	**83**
16.6km (10¼ miles)	2/3	5¼hrs	**87**
7km (4½ miles)	1	2¼hrs	**94**
13.4km (8¼ miles)	3/4	4½hrs	**99**
6.8km (4¼ miles)	4/5	4hrs	**104**
8.8km (5½ miles)	1/2	3¼hrs	**109**
6.9km (4¼ miles)	1	1¾hrs	**114**
14.3km (9 miles)	3/4	4¾hrs	**118**
7.1km (4½ miles)	2	2½hrs	**124**
14.2km (8¾ miles)	1/2	4¼hrs	**128**
16km (10 miles)	4	5hrs	**135**
13.5km (8½ miles)	3/4	4½hrs	**142**
9.3km (5¾ miles)	4	3½hrs	**147**
11.8km (7¼ miles)	3	3½hrs	**152**
11.6km (7¼ miles)	2	3½hrs	**158**
6.7km (4 miles)	2/3	2½hrs	**163**
9.5km (6 miles)	4	3hrs	**169**
11.3km (7 miles)	2	3hrs	**174**
9.2km (5¾ miles)	2	2¾hrs	**180**

Loughrigg Tarn with the Langdale Pikes behind (Walk 9)

Grisedale, just one of the Lake District's beautiful valleys (Walk 26)

INTRODUCTION

Hardened hill-walkers who head only for the highest ground of the Lake District may look down, both literally and figuratively, on people exploring the low fells and valleys, but in fact they're missing out on much of the natural beauty and drama of this National Park and UNESCO World Heritage Site. Head up onto the lower hills or take a walk through any of Lakeland's great dales, and you'll discover that they are gorgeous, often spectacular and atmospheric places where attention to detail in the landscape will reward the observant walker.

From delightful wooded glades and sparkling tarns hidden in green folds on the hillside to tumultuous waterfalls and glacier-carved valleys towered over by craggy mountains, this guide aims to seek out the best that the lower areas of the Lake District have to offer. It visits fascinating historical sights, completes circuits of some of the most striking lakes and climbs several smaller fells for breathtaking views.

Those who are new to walking in this much beloved corner of England will find gentle strolls (such as the circuit of Buttermere, Walk 18) as well as walks that provide a straightforward introduction to the low fells (such as High Rigg, Walk 23). Those who already know the Lake District National Park will enjoy a new take on Lakeland classics (such as Outerside and Barrow, Walk 24) and a chance to explore less well-known areas (such as Seathwaite Tarn, Walk 6). Hopefully, we'll also tempt some of those 'hardened hill-walkers' down from the tops!

GEOLOGY

The Lake District's rocks can be divided into six main types: Skiddaw slates, Borrowdale volcanics, Silurian slates, Coniston limestone, Carboniferous limestone and granite. They result in a surprisingly varied landscape for such a small area.

The Skiddaw slates are the oldest. Laid down by sedimentary processes almost 500 million years ago, they give rise to the smooth, rounded hills such as those of the Northern Fells. The Borrowdale volcanics were created about 450 million years ago. More resistant to erosion, they've created the high, craggy mountains of the central Lake District. Further south, the lower hills are made up of slates, siltstones and sandstones from the Silurian period, about 420 million years ago. Between the Borrowdale volcanics and the Silurian slates is a narrow band of limestone – known as Coniston limestone – stretching from the Duddon Estuary to Shap. Another area of limestone, dating from the Carboniferous period, and often creating limestone pavement, or karst scenery, forms a partial ring around the edge of Cumbria, including the south-east corner of the Lake District. The final group of rocks are the granite intrusions that appear in just a few places, including Eskdale.

Periods of catastrophic earth movements, as continents have collided throughout the earth's history,

Limestone pavement on Hampsfell (Walk 5)

Glaciers carved out deep valleys like this one at Langstrath

have helped shape the Lake District. The mountain-building event known as the Variscan orogeny, for instance, created the broad dome that gives the Lake District National Park its basic profile. But it is the action of ice during the last glacial period, which ended about 10,000 years ago, that created most of the surface features we see today. The glaciers that formed in the central part of the Lake District produced a radial drainage pattern. They gouged out deep, U-shaped valleys and created arêtes, waterfalls in hanging valleys and long, narrow lakes held back by debris dropped by the retreating ice. High in the mountains, the ice plucked out corries, or cirques, that are now home to tarns.

WILDLIFE AND HABITATS

In spite of hundreds of millions of years of geological upheaval, the Lake District is far from being a 'natural' landscape. The most common mammal you'll see on the walks in this book will be sheep. Mankind has been taming the mountains and valleys here for thousands of years. If they'd been left untouched, the fells would today be covered in a thick cloak of oak, birch and pine. Only the highest peaks would be visible, and

A roe deer in the woods above Grasmere

the valleys would be impenetrable swamps.

That's not to say there are no native species left. Ancient woodland consisting largely of sessile oak still exists, while stands of birch and alder remain on the damp ground in some valley bottoms. There are also rowan, holly, crab apple and witch-hazel as well as areas where Britain's only three native conifers – yew, juniper and Scots pine – can still be found.

Heathers, bilberry, lichen and mosses cover the fells, but there are wildflowers too in the woods and valley bottoms – red campion, lady's mantle, bog myrtle, spotted orchids, wood anemone, asphodels, bluebells and daffodils, of course. Rare orchids can be found on the limestone pavement, as can some of Britain's most endangered butterflies, including the high brown and pearl-bordered fritillaries.

The fells are home all year round to ravens, buzzards and peregrines. Ospreys have recently returned to breed during the summer and red kites have also been reintroduced. In the spring, you'll encounter a range of migratory species, including wheatear and ring ouzel on the fells and, lower down, redstart, pied flycatcher, wood warbler and tree pipit. Among the year-round valley residents are dippers, wagtails, chaffinches, great-spotted woodpeckers, nuthatches and sparrowhawks. With so many lakes, you'll inevitably come across large numbers of waterfowl too.

The Lake District's woods are home to roe deer, otters, badgers, voles, shrews, red squirrels, dormice and even the rare and elusive pine marten. You may occasionally catch sight of foxes, hares and stoats, while red deer tend to be confined to the higher fells.

HISTORY

The first solid evidence of human existence in the county we now call Cumbria comes from the Mesolithic period, between 10,000BC and 4500BC. Tiny flint chippings have been unearthed on the coast, proof that these hunter-gatherers made it this far north. But it was really only in Neolithic times that human beings, farming for the first time, began to have a more profound impact on the landscape. Suddenly, after centuries of being left to their own devices, the forests that had slowly colonised the land after the departure of the last ice sheets were under threat as trees made way for crops and livestock.

Neolithic and, later, Bronze Age people left their mark on the Lake District landscape in other ways too – in the form of stone circles. For more about Bronze Age remains, see Walk 30.

The Iron Age, starting in roughly 800BC in Britain and lasting up until the arrival of the Romans, introduced more sophisticated farming methods as well as the Celtic languages that feature in topographical place names in the area. *Blain* meaning summit, for example, gives rise to *blen* as in Blencathra. The most dramatic remains of the Celtic people are their hill forts at places such as Castle Crag (see Walk 22) and Carrock Fell near Caldbeck.

When the Romans arrived in Britain in AD43, the Celtic people of northern England, the Brigantes, made pacts with the invaders and

Remains of the Iron Age hill fort on Carrock Fell

were allowed to live autonomously for many years. Eventually, though, the deals broke down as the Brigantes began fighting among themselves, and the new rulers moved in to quash them. (See Walk 16 for more on the Romans.)

As in most of Britain, little is known about the period after the Romans left. These are the Dark Ages, when fact and fiction become intertwined and semi-mythological figures such as King Arthur and Urien of Rheged appear. The latter, famed for uniting northern Celtic kings against the Anglo-Saxons, is thought to have ruled over much of modern-day Cumbria.

Celtic rule began to decline in the early seventh century and, before long, the Anglo-Saxons held power in much of lowland Cumbria. In the uplands, however, it was the Norsemen who dominated. These settlers, of Scandinavian origin, began arriving from Ireland and the Isle of Man towards the end of the ninth century. Like the Celts, they left their mark on the modern map of Cumbria: the word fell, for instance, comes from the Norse *fjell*, meaning mountain.

After the Norman Conquest, Cumbria, like all of the border lands, entered a period of instability as territory passed from English rule to Scottish rule and back again. In the early part of the 14th century, Scottish raiders, led by Robert the

Bruce, ransacked much of the county – towns were burned, churches destroyed and villagers slaughtered. During a particularly grim period in their history, Cumbrians also had to cope with famines, the Black Death and the infamous Border Reivers – the lawless clans that went about the region looting and pillaging. Life really only began to settle down in 1603 when James VI of Scotland became the first ruler of both England and Scotland.

Trade and industry played an important role in the development of the Lake District from the 13th century onwards when wealthy monastic houses, most notably the Furness Cistercians, made money from the wool trade, brewing and coppicing. The latter resulted in timber as well as charcoal destined for the area's bloomeries, the earliest type of furnace to smelt iron from its oxides. Mineral exploitation took off in the 16th century when Elizabeth I invited German miners to come to England. The scars of their industry – and the subsequent operations which reached their peak in the 19th century – still litter the Lake District. (See Walk 21 for details.)

The mining and quarrying industries weren't the only activities to take advantage of the Lake District's natural resources. The area's abundant water, in the form of fast-flowing rivers and becks, allowed it to play a significant role in the textile industry too. While the wool industry, centred on Kendal, thrived from the 14th century onwards, during the Industrial Revolution the region's water-powered mills were providing bobbins for the huge cotton mills of Yorkshire and Lancashire. And, from the 18th century onwards, its landscape began generating money from tourism, a sector that got a big boost from the birth of the railways in the 19th century as well as a change in attitudes towards nature and the countryside.

WEATHER

Lying on Britain's west coast and subject to the whims of the prevailing south-westerlies coming in off the Atlantic, the Lake District experiences very changeable weather. There's no denying that Cumbria is wet – Borrowdale, in fact, holds the UK record for the highest rainfall in a 24-hour period – but that is only a fraction of the overall picture. The county is part of a windy, fast-moving scenario, which means the rain doesn't often linger. Spend a week in the Lake District, and you'd be unlucky if you had more than one day of heavy rain; a combination of sunshine and showers is more likely, and maybe even one or two days of brilliant blue skies.

Your best chance of dry weather is probably in May and June, but early spring and late autumn often hold

Autumn colours looking back towards Skiddaw on the last part of Walk 20

Caldbeck on the northern edge of the National Park

some pleasant surprises too. As in the rest of the UK, the warmest weather is in June, July and August, although temperatures are lower than in the south of England. The coldest months are January and February, and this is when high road passes such as Kirkstone, Wrynose and Hardknott can become blocked by snow.

The weather may not be a crucial factor for the valley walks in this book, but it is an important consideration when heading on to the fells. Get an accurate, mountain-specific weather forecast before setting out, such as that provided by the Mountain Weather Information Service (www.mwis.org.uk). The Lake District Weatherline (0844 846 2444 www.lakedistrictweatherline. co.uk) has five-day Met Office forecasts and, during the winter, provides information on fell-top conditions.

WHERE TO STAY

Tourism is a mainstay of the Lake District economy, so there's no shortage of beds, particularly at the middle and top end of the market. But the area's popularity means accommodation prices are relatively high. Budget travellers may want to consider youth hostels or camping. You're also more likely to find good quality bed and breakfast accommodation at reasonable prices in the less well-known towns and villages, places such as

Caldbeck at the base of the Northern Fells, Gosforth at the entrance to Wasdale and Ulverston in the south of the county. However, if you do choose to stay in places such as these on the edge of the National Park, be aware that crossing the Lake District on narrow, winding roads, often using high mountain passes, can be a time-consuming business, particularly in summer when the volume of traffic rises significantly.

The best bases for walks in this book are, inevitably, in the central honeypots, particularly Hawkshead, Coniston, Grasmere, Ambleside, Elterwater and Keswick or, for walks in the east, Glenridding.

For detailed information on accommodation, the Lake District's tourist information centres are a superb resource (see Appendix B), as is the official website of Cumbria Tourism – www.golakes.co.uk.

GETTING AROUND

Contrary to popular belief, the Lake District's main towns, villages and dales are well served by buses, although a few routes run only in summer. No rail lines penetrate far into the National Park: a branch line from Oxenholme links Windermere with the West Coast Main Line, and the Cumbria Coast and Furness lines run

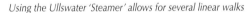

Using the Ullswater 'Steamer' allows for several linear walks

along the county's coast, flirting briefly with the Lake District at Grange-over-Sands and Ravenglass. Pick up a copy of one of Cumbria County Council's publications: the Travel Map and Guide for basic information or Go Cumbria for more detail. Alternatively, phone Traveline on 0871 200 2233 or visit www.traveline.org.uk.

Regular ferry services on the main lakes – Derwentwater, Ullswater, Windermere and Coniston Water – are also a useful facility for walkers.

WAYMARKING AND ACCESS

In terms of waymarking and access, the Lake District is as close to heaven as walkers get in England. As well as thousands of kilometres of bridleways and footpaths, there are huge tracts of 'access land' – mostly mountains, moor, heath and common land where people can walk without having to follow rights of way. Stiles, bridges, gates and, in the valleys, fingerposts, are well maintained. Path surfaces too, which suffer erosion due to the combined effects of walkers' boots and wet weather, are well looked after by a number of bodies.

A programme, known as Fix the Fells, repairs and maintains upland paths. Money for the work comes from a combination of donations and partner organisations, including the National Trust, the Lake District National Park Authority and the Friends of the Lake District. Visit www.fixthefells.co.uk for details on how to donate or volunteer.

Most of the walks in this book follow well-established paths, but you will need to consult your compass from time to time in less well-walked areas.

MAPS

The map extracts used in this book are from the Ordnance Survey's 1:50,000 Landranger series enlarged to 1:40,000 scale for maximum clarity. They are meant as a guide only and walkers are advised to purchase the relevant map(s) – and know how to navigate using them. The whole area is covered by sheets 89, 90, 96 and 97. The OS 1:25,000 Explorer series provides greater detail, showing field boundaries as well as access land. To complete all the walks in this guide using Explorer maps, you'll need sheets OL4, OL5, OL6 and OL7.

Harvey publishes an excellent series of Superwalker XT25 maps at the 1:25,000 scale. Its four Lake District maps cover most of the National Park.

DOGS

Dog owners should always be sensitive to the needs of livestock and wildlife. The law states that dogs have to be controlled so that they do not scare or disturb livestock or wildlife, including

Looking across Little Langdale Tarn to Wetherlam and Swirl How (Walk 7)

ground-nesting birds. On open access land, they have to be kept on leads of no more than 2m long from 1 March to 31 July – and all year round near sheep. A dog chasing lambing sheep can cause them to abort. Remember that, as a last resort, farmers can shoot dogs to protect their livestock.

Cattle, particularly cows with calves, may very occasionally pose a risk to walkers with dogs. If you ever feel threatened by cattle, you should let go of your dog's lead and let it run free.

CLOTHING, EQUIPMENT AND SAFETY

The amount of gear you take on a walk and the clothes you wear will differ according to the length of the route, the time of year and the terrain you're likely to encounter. Preparing for Tarn Crag in the height of winter, for example, requires more thought than setting out on the circuit of Buttermere. This section is aimed at those heading out in the winter or venturing on to higher ground.

Even in the height of summer, your daysack should contain everything you need to make yourself wind and waterproof. Most people will also carry several layers of clothing – this is more important if you are heading on to higher ground where the weather is prone to sudden change.

As far as footwear goes, some walkers like good, solid leather boots with plenty of ankle support while others prefer something lighter. Whatever you wear, make sure it has a good grip and isn't likely to result in a twisted ankle on uneven ground.

Every walker needs to carry a map and compass – and know how to use them. Always take food and water with you – enough to sustain you during the walk and extra rations in case you're out for longer than originally planned. Emergency equipment should include a whistle and a torch – the distress signal being six flashes/whistle-blasts repeated at one-minute intervals. Pack a small first aid kit too.

Carry a fully charged mobile telephone, but use it to summon help on the hills only in a genuine emergency. If things do go badly wrong and you need help, first make sure you have a note of all the relevant details such as your location, the nature of the injury/problem, the number of people in the party and your mobile phone number. Only then should you dial 999 and ask for Cumbria Police, then mountain rescue.

USING THIS GUIDE

The routes in this book cover the whole of the Lake District and are divided into five sections: South Lakes, Central Lakes, Western Valleys, North Lakes and Eastern Lakes. Most are circular, but there are a few linear walks that make use of the area's buses and boats. Check timetables carefully to make sure you have enough time to complete the route.

Each walk description contains information on start/finish points; distance covered; total ascent; grade; approximate walking time; terrain; maps required; refreshments; and public transport options. The walks are graded one to five, one being the easiest.

Please note that these ratings are subjective: based not just on distance and total ascent, but also on the type of terrain. So, whereas one 5-mile walk with 1200ft of ascent might be graded 'one'; another of the same length with the same amount of ascent might be graded 'two' if walkers are likely to encounter a lot of rough or boggy ground. Walkers are advised to read route descriptions in full before setting out to get a sense of what to expect. It might be an idea to do an easy walk first and then judge the rest accordingly. The route summary table on pages 6 and 7 will help you make your choice.

SOUTH LAKES
Windermere, Coniston,
Duddon and the south

Tarn Beck (Walk 6)

Walk 1

Tarn Hows and the Monk Coniston Estate

*The delightful low-lying countryside to the north of Coniston contains
a vast amount of variety and interest. From the peaceful shores of
Coniston Water and the waterfalls of Tom Gill through to Monk Coniston's
walled gardens and arboretum, the scenery is constantly changing. The
highlight of the day, however, has to be Tarn Hows with its beautiful
mountain backdrop. This popular beauty spot is reached about halfway
through the walk, so it makes a great place to stop for a picnic.*

Returning to Coniston through the woods

Start/finish	Monk Coniston pay-and-display car park at the N end of Coniston Water (SD 316 978)
Distance	10.3km (6½ miles)
Total ascent	455m (1490ft)
Grade	2
Walking time	3½hrs
Terrain	Field paths, some unclear; woodland trails; surfaced tracks; roadside path
Maps	OS Explorer OL7; or OS Landrangers 96 and 90
Refreshments	Choice of pubs and cafés in Coniston
Transport	Bus 505

From the car park entrance, cross the road and turn left along the walkway. At the T-junction, cross over, go through the gap in the hedge opposite and turn left to continue along the roadside path. After passing the **Waterhead Hotel**, you have an uninterrupted view of the mountains, including the gnarled face of the Old Man. Soon after the walkway ends, turn right along Shepherds Bridge Lane on the edge of Coniston – signposted Skelwith and Ambleside.

Turn right to cross the old bridge soon after the entrance to Coniston Primary School on the other side of the road. (This is not the bridge into the sports centre car park.) The path goes left before some white gates and enters a field. The way ahead is obvious as far as a large gate. Don't go through this; instead, keep to the right of the wall/fence to reach a stone folly, built by local landowner James Marshall as a kennel and now a National Trust information shelter. Once through the gate here, the route is more obvious again.

Soon after the next gate, keep left at a waymarked fork. After a short section of woodland, you are greeted by an impressive vista of the Yewdale

Tarn Hows with a snow-topped Wetherlam behind

Fells. The clear path soon runs out;
continue parallel with the wall on
your right and then swing half-left
at a waymarker post to go
through a gate. Keep to the
highest ground through
the next field and
then drop to a

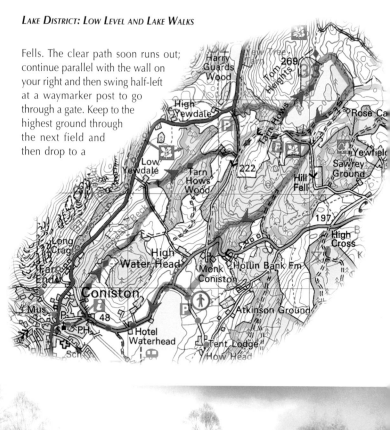

kissing-gate beside a rough track, along which you turn left – signposted Tarn Hows.

Just before the bridge over **Yewdale Beck**, go through the kissing-gate on the right and walk with the fence on your left. Beyond the next gate, the path continues beside the beck for a short while before climbing through **Tarn Hows Wood**. Keep to the permitted route to the right of Tarn Hows Cottage and then turn right along the rough track to reach a minor road.

Since leaving Coniston, you've been following the Cumbria Way – a long-distance path that links Ulverston in the south of the county with Carlisle in the north. You part company with it here: while the Cumbria Way goes left along the road to take the quick, easy way to Tarn Hows, we follow a longer, but more interesting and attractive route beside Tom Gill. So, step on to the road, but then turn sharp left to descend a stony track beside the wall.

Bear right to enter the National Trust's Tom Gill car park. Just before the road, take the path on the right – beside the pay-and-display machine. Cross the bridge and turn right. A lovely path now heads gently uphill through mostly deciduous woodland beside Tom Gill. At one point, there is a steep, unfenced drop to your right, so watch your footing. The main waterfall is now clearly visible as a slender, white plume through the trees. The path goes almost to the base of it and then climbs. After a gate, continue with the beck on your right to reach the wide path at the edge of peaceful **Tarn Hows**. Turn left to begin a circuit of the tarn.

Patchy ice on Tarn Hows on a cold winter's morning

James Garth Marshall, a Leeds industrialist, bought the **Monk Coniston estate** in 1835. Tarn Hows was originally three tiny tarns, but Marshall dammed one of them to create the single tarn that exists today. He also planted the conifer plantations that surround it, intending both to frame and reveal views of his new creation. His plans were based on the ideas of the 'picturesque' that were popular at the time.

In 1926, as the Marshall family fortunes declined, the house and gardens were sold. The rest of the estate, including all the farmland and Tarn Hows, was purchased by the author Beatrix Potter in 1930. She immediately sold half at cost price to the National Trust; the other half passed to the charity after her death in 1943. In 1945 the National Trust purchased the hall and gardens, reuniting the estate once more.

The path winds its way round the tarn in a surprisingly roller-coaster fashion – sometimes along the water's edge; sometimes with snatched glimpses of it through the trees. On reaching a fingerpost, keep straight on – signposted Hawkshead. Swinging round the eastern side of the tarn, above **Rose Castle Plantation**, you reach another junction of paths. Keep straight on again – signposted Coniston. The finest views of the tarn – with Wetherlam and the Coniston Fells forming a grand backdrop – are revealed from this high promenade.

Having almost completed a circuit of the tarn, the path forks. Bear left here for a surprise glimpse of the Langdale Pikes in the distance. Just after a bench, step off the path and on to the road above. Turn left along the asphalt. Drawing level with a small National Trust car park on the left, you'll see several gates on your right. The first of these provides access to a field. Go through the second gate. This leads into the forest – signposted Coniston.

Walking with the wall on your right, bear right at an early fork. Descend steadily to reach a wider path, and bear left along it. Go right at a fork a few metres further on. Ignore a couple of faint routes off; simply keep to the clear path until, a few metres after crossing a beck, you see some steps on the left – signposted Monk Coniston. Descend these and follow the path down to a minor road. Go through the gate opposite.

A clear path leads to a junction. Keep left, soon entering the walled garden of **Monk Coniston**. Walk into the middle of the garden and turn right, exiting via another gate in a wall. Keep left to descend between exotic trees to reach a gate on the edge of the arboretum. Once through this, follow the grassy path in the general direction of Coniston Water. On reaching the road, cross over to return to the car park where the walk started.

Tarn Hows with the Coniston Fells behind

Walk 2

Kelly Hall Tarn and Coniston Water

Easily reached from Torver, Kelly Hall Tarn lies hidden on low moorland above Coniston Water and is a superb spot from which to view the nearby mountains, including Dow Crag and Coniston Old Man. Beyond the tarn, the walk continues across the often pathless moorland before dropping to the shores of the lake for an easy stroll north in tranquil surroundings. After flirting with the edge of Coniston village, it picks up the route of a disused railway and follows this almost all the way back to Torver.

The route begins to descend towards Coniston Water

Start/finish	Torver village hall car park (SD 284 943)
Distance	11.3km (7 miles)
Total ascent	185m (610ft)
Grade	1/2
Walking time	3hrs
Terrain	Farm tracks; low-lying, often pathless moorland; lakeside trail; disused railway
Maps	OS Explorer OL6; or OS Landranger 96
Refreshments	Church House Inn and Wilson Arms, both in Torver
Transport	Bus X12

From the car park entrance, turn left along the road, soon passing the **church**. Take the next road on the left – signposted Greenodd, Ulverston and Lancaster. After just 100m, turn right along a rough track set back slightly from the road. It passes to the left of a detached house.

A few metres after passing a tiny campsite, take the track on the left. When this bends right, leave it by going through the gate on the left – signposted Mill Bridge and Stable Harvey.

Follow this clear path to reach The Mill on Torver Beck. Cross the bridge here and turn left along a path that climbs gently to the **A5084**.

Turn right along the road and, in about 100m, you'll reach the garage of Lakeland Land Rover. Opposite this is what looks like a large gravel parking area.

At the back of this, there is a muddy track that soon passes through a gate providing access to **Torver Back Common**. Bear left along the grassy path. Keeping to the reasonably wide route, you'll soon see a small pool on the

The Coniston Fells from Kelly Hall Tarn

right. This is Kelly Hall Tarn, a lovely spot to linger and enjoy the views across to the Coniston Fells.

About 300m beyond Kelly Hall Tarn, you'll see another small tarn ahead: Long Moss. Keep left at the fork here.

The onward route becomes less obvious now: trend right on to the high ground and then, with only the faintest of paths to guide you, swing right again (north north-east) to reach the unmarked top of this part of the common. The views from here include the Coniston Fells, with Dow Crag looking particularly impressive, and Coniston Water. Heading north-east, pick up a grassy trail along the top of this low ridge, running parallel with the wall to the left. Keep right when this forks – now descending towards the lake.

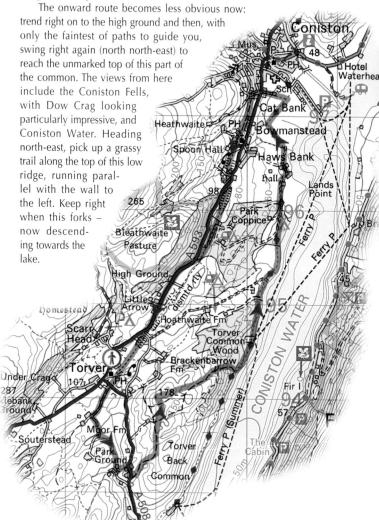

FORESTRY: FROM WAR EFFORT TO LEISURE

On the eastern shore of Coniston Water – and stretching almost as far as the waters of Windermere in places – is Grizedale, Cumbria's largest area of forest. Covering almost 25 square kilometres, it does contain several areas of deciduous species, even some ancient woodland, but much of it consists of dense conifer plantations planted in the early 20th century. By the end of World War One, Britain's woodland resources were severely depleted, particularly by trench warfare, so there was a pressing need to rebuild and maintain a strategic timber reserve. The Forestry Act came into force on 1 September 1919 and the new Forestry Commission was given a lot of freedom to acquire land. The Commission's first planting in the Lake District was at Hospital Plantation, close to Whinlatter Pass, in 1919.

By the second half of the 20th century, these dark forests with their regimented lines of conifers were hugely unpopular. The guidebook writer Alfred Wainwright described Ennerdale's trees, for instance, as being 'deformed, crowded in a battery, denied light and air and natural growth'.

Today, the Forestry Commission still carries out commercial harvesting, but its role has changed. It is increasingly involved with conservation, and in some places (including Ennerdale) the conifers are being replaced by native species. Tourism has also become an important part of the forest economy with visitors to Lake District forests drawn by many kilometres of walking trails, sculpture trails, mountain biking routes, children's adventure playgrounds and tree-top climbing courses.

Looking across to the Coniston Fells from Torver Back Common

Soon after entering an area of juniper, the path heads left to drop off the ridge. At the bottom of the slope, continue parallel with the wall. You'll quickly encounter a clearer path crossing the beck. Ignoring this, continue with the beck on your left for now and then go through a gate on the edge of the woods. Follow the trail down through the trees to reach the shores of **Coniston Water**.

Go left at the water's edge, soon passing through a small gate. The route through the trees isn't obvious at first, but keep close to the lake and you shouldn't go wrong. Just after passing a boating centre, go through a gate close to the edge of a campsite. Bear right here – ignoring the clear track – and quickly pass through another gate to regain the lakeshore.

After an open, grassy area with magnificent views of the Coniston Fells, go through a gate to join a broad track. This now takes you away from the water's edge. The track passes to the left of Coniston Hall, a 16th-century house with distinctive cylindrical chimneys.

After a gate between two stone farm buildings, turn right along a gravel path. About 100m before the path reaches some white buildings, go through the double gates on the left. You are now standing next to the school playing fields. Go through a large wooden gate about 40m to your left. This provides access to an enclosed grassy path which, in turn, leads to a surfaced lane. Follow this to the main road and carefully cross over to head up the narrow lane opposite. This winds its way steeply uphill.

About 150m beyond the main road, as the lane performs a sharp bend to the left, go through the gap in the wall to the right of the asphalt. You are now standing on the old trackbed of the Coniston branch line of the former Furness Railway. Turn left along the disused line.

This **branch line** of the Furness Railway was opened in 1859 to link Coniston with the main line at Broughton. It must have come as a relief to the managers of the Coniston Mining Company, who had previously had to arrange for ore and slate from the copper mines and quarries to be moved by barge down the lake or by horse and cart to the Ulverston Canal.

As you'd expect of a railway path, the next stretch of the route is straightforward and requires little effort, allowing you to appreciate the lovely woods and occasional glimpses of the lake. After about 900m, the permitted path ends at a lane. Turn left here and then go right along the main road. After another 70m, go through the gate on the left – signposted Torver. Now pick up the route of the old railway again, the path running along the bottom of a shallow ditch. Soon after two gates in quick succession, bear right along Park Coppice caravan site's access lane.

When this swings right, take the track on the left, soon going through a small gate. When this track ends, go through the gate up to the right and then turn left along a gravel path running parallel with the road.

About 800m along this roadside path, it drops through a gate on the left. Before long, you are walking along another section of the old railway that's been converted to path. Ignoring a trail up to the right shortly after joining it, follow the railway path all the way to a road. Now turn right and then right again at the T-junction in Torver. The car park where the walk started is about 200m ahead on the right.

Walk 3
Swinside Stone Circle

The impressive Swinside Stone Circle, also known as Sunkenkirk, lies in the far south-west corner of the Lake District in a landscape of low grassy fells and occasional craggy knobbles divided by rough grazing land. This tightly clustered, small circle of surprisingly large stones is a bit off the beaten track as far as sightseers go, and yet it can hold its own among the Cumbrian heavyweights such as Castlerigg.

The ancient stones of Swinside Stone Circle

Start/finish	Bridge over Black Beck (SD 180 877) on a minor road about 2.4km N of Hallthwaites. From Duddon Bridge on the A595, take the road heading N along the W side of the River Duddon. After 3.5km, take the turning on the left for Millom. The bridge is about 1.8km along this road. There is room for two or three cars beside the road here.
Distance	7.6km (4¾ miles)
Total ascent	250m (810ft)
Grade	2
Walking time	2¾hrs
Terrain	Stony tracks; pathless moorland, boggy in places; field paths; quiet road
Maps	OS Explorer OL6; or OS Landranger 96
Refreshments	None en route
Transport	Buses 7/7B and, in the summer, the X33 pass along the A595, about 1km from the start of the Swinside farm track

From the bridge, walk south along the quiet lane for about 400m. Soon after passing **Cragg Hall**, take the farm track on the right – signposted Swinside Stone Circle. After crossing a cattle grid, you lose the enclosing walls. Nearing the farm buildings at **Swinside**, you'll see the stone circle straight ahead. Soon after the next cattle grid, a wooden gate on the right allows access to the field containing this prehistoric enigma.

After visiting the stone circle, continue towards the farm on the track. It swings left to pass

Looking across to the farmhouse at Fenwick from near Swinside

to the left of the buildings. There's a sign indicating a footpath to the right imme-diately after the farm, but you should keep straight ahead on the bridleway. This passes to the right of some sheepfolds and through a gate at the base of the fells.

Swinside Stone Circle dates from the early Bronze Age. It consists of 55 stones, all local slate, set tightly in a 30m-diameter ring. As in other stone circles in Cumbria, a gap to the south-east of the ring forms an entrance, marked by two large outer portal stones. The name Sunkenkirk comes from a local legend claiming that, every night, the Devil would pull down the stones of a church that was being built on the site.

The rough track swings right, through another gate, and heads uphill. The rocky ground on the left belongs to Raven Crag, while the views over the wall on your right include the Coniston range, Bow Fell and the Scafells. The going underfoot is good at first, but then, as the wall on the right turns to fence, things get trickier. As the clear path ends, cross a tributary beck. Continue in roughly the same direction (north-west) – parallel with the main beck down to your right. There are faint signs of a track on the ground, but you'll need to bypass its boggier sections. The important thing is not to lose or gain too much height just yet. Only after about 400m of this rough-going does the path swing slightly left and begin gently ascending.

You'll see a ruined building on the other side of the beck: make your way towards it. Go through a wooden gate on the southern side of the stream, carefully ford the channel and then head up through the long grass and bracken to another gate behind the ruin. It's now less than 500m to the fell road, but you have to cross some damp, tussocky ground to reach it – and there's no path to guide you. So, set your compass to north north-west, take a deep breath and strike out across the moss.

Turn right at the road. About 200m after crossing a beck, you reach a fingerpost at the crest of a rise. Turn right here (south-east). Again, there is no path on the ground, although you may be lucky enough to find a sheep trod heading in your direction. If your compass reading is good, you'll reach a gate in a wall about 350m from the road. It has a 'no cycling' sign on it.

Go through this gate and walk down to a fingerpost in the meadow. The post marks a junction of paths: the clearer of the two heads right, but you want the less walked path – signposted Duddon Bridge. This descends through the long grass (east south-east). Cross a stile in a wall about 80m to the left of the white farmhouse at **Fenwick**. (This is not easy to spot from above). Bear right and aim for the far corner of this field, crossing a stile in the wall a few metres to the left of a telegraph pole.

A few more strides bring you to a farm track, along which you turn left. Passing some barns in a dip at **Windy Slack** along the way, follow this track to a road, then turn right.

With the massive expanse of the Duddon Estuary providing the visual entertainment for much of the way, there is now about 1.2km of downhill walking to return to the bridge where the walk started.

The Coniston fells are often visible on this route

Walk 4

Claife Heights, Windermere and Latterbarrow

This lovely, varied route to the west of Windermere combines a lakeshore track with forest paths and trails, and visits two superbly located tarns as well as the 245m summit of Latterbarrow for some superb 360-degree views. Take your time: enjoy the scenery and don't forget to turn round every now and then to appreciate the vista behind you – the meandering nature of this walk means the scenes are constantly changing.

The central fells provide a spectacular backdrop to Wise Een Tarn

Start/finish	Pay-and-display car park in Hawkshead. The walk starts from the larger of the two to the S (SD 353 980)
Distance	16.7km (10.4 miles)
Total ascent	680m (2228ft)
Grade	3
Walking time	5¼hrs
Terrain	Quiet lanes; forest tracks/trails; field paths; low, grassy fell
Maps	OS Explorer OL7; or OS Landrangers 96 and 90
Refreshments	Choice of cafés and pubs in Hawkshead; Cuckoo Brow Inn and Frithy's tearoom in Far Sawrey
Transport	Bus 505 and, in the summer, the 525 and X30

From the entrance to the larger of the two pay-and-display car parks in Hawkshead, turn right along the road – away from the village. After going right at the T-junction, turn left at the next junction and then, soon after a small bridge, take the lane on the left – signposted Wray.

Ignoring a turning on the right, follow the road up through **Colthouse**. When you see the gated driveway of **Gillbank** to the right of the asphalt, turn sharp right – almost back on yourself – through a tall wooden gate. Ignoring a faint trail to the left early on, keep to the well-walked path for about 1.7km, heading deeper into the forest and climbing steadily all the while. The path splits on a couple of occasions, but it doesn't matter which branch you take. On reaching a junction in a clearing, turn right – signposted Far Sawrey.

Another 450m or so brings you to the next waymarked junction. Turn right, along a stony trail heading uphill. On emerging on the wide forest track, bear right.

The Fairfield Horseshoe seen from the climb on to Latterbarrow

After a small gate at the edge of the trees, the route drops between a small tarn on the left and the larger **Wise Een Tarn** over to the right. The path becomes less clear as it descends on grass, but there is a waymarker.

Take a moment, as you pass
Wise Een Tarn, to enjoy
the spectacular

The shores of Windermere

view. This is a sublime location with the mountains of Langdale providing a truly beautiful backdrop to this otherwise unexciting body of water. Beyond the tarn, continue on a clear track through a gate and then down to **Moss Eccles Tarn**.

Moss Eccles Tarn is a Site of Special Scientific Interest, with its interesting aquatic plants, damselflies and dragonflies. It was bought by Beatrix Potter in 1913. She and her husband kept a boat on the tarn and spent many summer evenings here.

Continue descending between drystone walls. At a clear fork, bear left through a gate – signposted Far Sawrey. Bear right along a surfaced lane, which leads to the road through Far Sawrey. Turn left and walk along the asphalt for about 200m. Immediately after the telephone box opposite the entrance to the Braithwaite Hall car park, there are two tracks to the left of the road. Take the first of these, almost heading back on yourself – signposted Belle Grange.

After a gate, bear right at a fork. After the next gate, keep straight on – signposted Windermere lakeshore. Ignoring any paths to the right, descend through the mixed woodland on a clear, stony track. Catching glimpses of Windermere through the trees as you lose height, you eventually drop to the lakeshore track, along which you turn left.

Keep straight on at a path junction after 1.9km of easy walking beside Windermere, to pass the white house of **Belle Grange**. On reaching the end of a surfaced lane, you'll see the **Red Nab** car park on your right. Go through this to pick up the continuation of the lakeshore route – signposted Wray Castle.

About 1.5km beyond the car park, having enjoyed some superb views across the lake towards Wansfell and the fells above Ambleside, you reach a boathouse on the edge of **High Wray Bay**. (This is the second boathouse since the car park.) Go through the kissing-gate on the left – signposted High Wray. Walking with the wall/fence on your right and going through one kissing-gate along the way, head uphill to reach a tiny gated stile in the top corner. Once through this, go right to reach the road.

Turn left and walk along the asphalt for about 200m – through High Wray. Just before **High Wray Farm**, take the broad track on the left – signposted Claife Heights. Bear right at a fork, the left-hand branch heading into the National Trust's Basecamp. Go through a gate and, about 100m beyond this, bear right along a narrow, waymarked trail. This soon crosses a stile and fords a small beck. The stony path climbs steadily through the trees to a kissing-gate. Beyond this, the gradient increases for the final and steepest climb of the day up bracken-covered slopes to the top of **Latterbarrow**.

The summit of **Latterbarrow** is marked by an enormous obelisk. From here, you have excellent 360-degree views that include the Coniston Fells, Bow Fell, the Langdale Pikes, Fairfield, the South-Eastern Fells, the Howgills and the Pennines.

From the obelisk, turn right, ignoring a narrower trail through the bracken to the right early on. Nearing the bottom of the slope, join a path from the left and continue to the road. Turn left along the asphalt and take the next road on the right. About 600m along this lane, you'll see a kissing-gate next to a double gate on your left. (This is the second of two signposted footpaths in quick succession.) Go through this gate and walk beside the fence/hedgerow on your right. Go through a kissing-gate and then continue along the field edge with the hedgerow now on your left.

After a couple of kissing-gates, you reach a fenced track, along which you turn left. This is Scar House Lane. Go through the next kissing-gate on your right – signposted Hawkshead. Follow the surfaced path, a shared pedestrian walkway and cycle path, through a gate and down to Black Beck. Joining another path from the right, turn left – beside the beck. After crossing the bridge, the path leads on to a track – turn left along it and go left again at the road. The car park where the walk started is up the lane on your right in another 200m.

BEATRIX POTTER AND THE NATIONAL TRUST

Beatrix Potter is best known for her illustrated children's books, but she was also a farmer and a conservationist whose legacy continues to play an enormous role in the National Trust's work in the Lake District.

Beatrix, originally from Kensington, first came to the Lakes in 1882, when her family spent a summer at Wray Castle on the shores of Windermere, close to Latterbarrow. As a young woman, when her family took a summer home near Hawkshead, she used to wander these hills sketching and, no doubt, coming up with ideas for her stories.

Later in life, having married a local solicitor, William Heelis, she used the royalties from her book sales to buy farmland. She was particularly passionate about Herdwicks, the hardy sheep that graze the fells. It is partly down to her and the efforts of her friend Canon Hardwicke Rawnsley, co-founder of the National Trust, that the breed still exists today. When she died in 1943, Beatrix Potter left 14 farms and more than 1600 hectares of land to the National Trust.

Today, the National Trust protects a massive 50,000 hectares of land in the Lake District – more than a quarter of the total area covered by the National Park. Huge expanses of the high fells, 24 lakes and tarns and much of their shorelines, 90 tenanted farms, 59 listed buildings, almost all of Borrowdale and other major valley heads are owned or held on lease by the charity. The Trust owns the bed of England's deepest lake – Wastwater – as well as the summit of England's highest mountain – Scafell Pike.

Walk 5

Hampsfell

Sometimes, the biggest views can be enjoyed from the smallest fells. That is definitely true of the tiny limestone hill of Hampsfell. Located on the southern edge of the National Park, its 222m summit provides fantastic views across Morecambe Bay as well as of the Lake District fells and the nearby Pennines. This walk explores Eggerslack Wood on the edge of Grange-over-Sands before climbing to the top, where a surprise awaits… Squatting in the middle of the limestone pavement is the Hampsfell Hospice, an entertaining Victorian shelter that makes a great spot for a picnic.

Looking back across the Kent estuary during the climb onto Hampsfell

Start/finish	Grange-over-Sands railway station (SD 412 781)
Distance	6.5km (4 miles)
Total ascent	285m (935ft)
Grade	2
Walking time	2¼hrs
Terrain	Pavement through town; woodland paths; low, grassy hill; exposed limestone may be slippery when wet
Maps	OS Explorer OL7; or OS Landranger 96 or 97
Refreshments	Choice of pubs and cafés in Grange-over-Sands
Transport	Buses 530, 532 and X6; Barrow–Lancaster railway line

Turn left out of the station car park and then go right at the mini-roundabout – along the **B5271** towards Newby Bridge and Ulverston. About 350m up this road, go through a gap in the wall on the left to enter Eggerslack Wood – signposted Hampsfield. A path, composed partly of exposed limestone, climbs through the trees. Cross straight over a surfaced lane, but then turn right at the next junction. Losing just a little of the height gained so far, this rough track ends near some houses close to the B5271. Turn left just before the road and then, soon after a cottage, keep right at a fork.

Immediately after fording a small beck, the path forks again. Bear left here, along the wider of the routes. Ignore a couple of narrower trails to the left and then the right as the path continues through the delightfully dense woodland. On reaching a T-junction next to a waymarker post, go left and leave the woods via a gate.

Turn left along a faint track beside the wall, soon going through a gate next to a ladder stile. This restricted byway skirts the base of the Bishop's or Tithe Allotment, just one of the walled sections of Hampsfell. Up to the right, limestone outcrops are scattered over the open hillside.

The Victorian hospice on Hampsfell

Having walked the byway for about 550m, you'll see a stile in the wall on the left. Turn right here to begin your climb to the top of **Hampsfell** – signposted The Hospice. The gradient is not at all strenuous and there is grass underfoot all the while, making it a pleasant ascent with time to savour the limestone scenery and the views.

To the left, **Arnside Knott** stands out on the other side of the Kent Estuary with the Forest of Bowland in the distance; looking further north, you can see the Yorkshire Dales, the Howgills and the Lake District fells.

Cross the allotment wall via a stile and turn sharp right. Follow the line of the wall at first, but when it bends right, keep straight ahead (west). In a few more metres, you'll see **the Hospice** ahead. Pick your way across the limestone pavement to reach it.

The Hospice was built in 1846 by the vicar of Cartmel. Entertaining panels inside invite the weary traveller to rest, enjoy the views and 'not by acts of wanton mischief and destruction show that they possess more muscle than brain'. A set of steps up the side of the shelter leads to a roof with an interesting viewfinder on it. Visitors can line up the arrow on the top with the angles given on a board to identify what they are looking at. The amazing panorama includes Blackpool Tower, Ingleborough, the Isle of Man, Coniston Old Man, Scafell and Skiddaw.

From the summit, head south south-west on a grassy path towards a large cairn on the edge of the limestone pavement.

The large church down in the next valley is the 12th-century **Cartmel Priory**. It survived the worst ravages of the Dissolution because, as well as being a monastery, it served as a parish church.

Descend to a stile in a wall, beyond which the grassy path continues across the broad crest of the hill. Nearing a dip, bear right at a fork and then continue climbing beyond the dip.

Dropping back into Grange-over-Sands at the end of the walk

As the ground ahead begins dropping away again, the views across the bay are truly magnificent. After crossing a wall stile next to a gate, bear half-left (south-east) on a faint path skirting the north-east edge of **Fell End**. Heading gently downhill, keep left at a waymarker post just beyond some piles of shattered limestone.

Turn left along the lane at the bottom of the slope. After about 150m, turn right – making for the grey farmhouse straight ahead. Follow the lane round to the left. On reaching the farm buildings, go right and then cross the stile in the wall on the left. A path heads up the right-hand side of the field and then drops to a stile. Once over this, follow the path round to a junction of roads on the edge of Grange-over-Sands.

Turn left along the narrow, private road. Keep straight on to reach Eden Mount Close, where you go right. Turn left at the T-junction, along Charney Well Lane. At the bottom of the initial slope, take the left turn – effectively straight on. With grand views out across the sands to Arnside Knott, this narrow lane drops to a T-junction. Turn left here and walk along Hampsfell Road for about 60m. Then take the surfaced path on the right leading into the trees.

Emerging on a narrow lane, turn right and drop to the main road. Turn left here, soon passing a couple of tearooms, including the award-winning Hazelmere Café. Go right at the mini-roundabout to return to the railway station.

Walk 6
Seathwaite Tarn

Sitting at the western foot of the gnarly Coniston Fells, Seathwaite Tarn lies in an out-of-the-way spot above lonely Dunnerdale. Reaching this crag-bound tarn at 373m above sea level involves crossing some rough, sometimes pathless, often boggy ground. But, with the scenery growing in grandeur all the time and a wonderful sense of remoteness building with every step taken, it's well worth the effort.

Crag-bound Seathwaite Tarn

Start/finish	Forestry Commission Birks Bridge car park beside the River Duddon, 2.8km S of Cockley Beck Bridge (SD 235 995)
Distance	9.8km (6 miles)
Total ascent	405m (1336ft)
Grade	3/4
Walking time	3½hrs
Terrain	Forest trails; low fell, often boggy, sometimes pathless; several fords, including two that may be difficult after heavy rain; section of road
Maps	OS Explorer OL6; or OS Landranger 96
Refreshments	Newfield Inn, Seathwaite, 4km S of Birks Bridge
Transport	None

Leaving the car park, turn left along the road. After about 500m, take the footpath on the right – the second path signposted on this side of the road. Cross the stile at the top of the short slope and follow the path heading steadily uphill. This soon goes straight across an old, grassed-over forestry track. It enters the woods and descends to a beck. Keeping this on your left for now, make your way over to the wall on the right. Carefully ford the beck here.

Having crossed a stile and a gap in a wall, turn left to climb

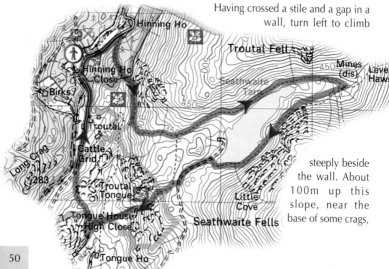

steeply beside the wall. About 100m up this slope, near the base of some crags,

Seathwaite Tarn's dam

the faint path swings right, away from the wall for a short while. Briefly emerging from the bracken at a boggy area, you'll see the wall up to your left again. The continuation of the path isn't easy to find when the bracken is high: as you cross the tiny beck here, the continuing trail is slightly lower than where you originally came out of the vegetation.

After rejoining the wall, follow its line for about 400m. Go through a small gate in the wall and bear half-right on a rising grassy trail. Hugging the base of some small crags, this swings left and climbs more steeply.

As the craggy, bouldery slopes of the Coniston Fells appear ahead, the path hits a boggy area. Bear left at a waymarker, skirting the worst of the dampness, but don't head too high: the general direction of travel continues to be east, following **Tarn Beck** upstream, so you need to watch for where the path swings right again. Seathwaite Tarn is a natural tarn that was enlarged in 1904 when it was dammed to supply drinking water for the Furness area.

The path becomes unclear as you near Seathwaite Tarn's dam. The trick is to keep reasonably high to avoid the worst of the boggy ground, but without heading up on to the hill. Beyond the dam, you'll see a tiny island on this side of the tarn. Aim for this and you'll find a path just back from the water's edge. Follow this towards the head of the valley where the steep slopes of Brim Fell and Swirl How tumble dramatically into the cirque.

The path continues beyond the end of the tarn – keeping a few metres above a large boggy area and, at one point, traversing a boulder slope. After passing a spoil heap – the remains of a 19th-century mine – the path drops and melts away in the morass. Keep to the edge of the wet ground, boulder-hopping where necessary. On encountering slightly drier ground – after passing a drystone construction on the other side of the beck – bear right at a fork. Carefully ford the beck and make your way downstream towards the drystone construction, crossing another channel along the way. The copper mines nearby get a mention in Richard Adams's 1977 book *The Plague Dogs*. The main characters, fugitive dogs Rowf and Snitter, use it as a hiding place.

Because of the crags and boulders littering the south-east shore of Seathwaite Tarn, the return follows a higher line than the outward route. There is no path across this rough ground at first, but if you head south-west for about 230m, climbing all the while, you'll pick up a faint trail along the 420m contour. Turn right along this. It makes light work of the rough, boulder-strewn slopes, later descending to the reservoir's south-west shore.

Becoming less clear in its later stages, the trail makes its way towards the southern end of the dam. Just beyond this, you'll find a clear track, along which you turn left.

After about 500m, the track swings left. Leave it here by turning right at a small waymarker. The grassy path heads downhill. After going through a gated gap in a wall close to a sheepfold, the path swings right. Cross the small beck and continue downstream.

After the next gate, the path crosses damp ground where bog asphodel and spotted orchids grow in the summer. After one more gate, make your way over to the ladder stile in the wall on the right. Climb this and turn left to cross the footbridge over Tarn Beck.

A faint path heads left and through a gate to skirt the edge of a wood. As it climbs away from the beck, take a faint, easy-to-miss trail climbing through the trees on the right. (If you reach a building at the edge of the trees, you've gone too far.) This crosses a tumbledown wall and heads north north-west (veering north) through the bracken on **High Tongue**. It goes through a gap in a wall and, with occasional views of Bow Fell and Crinkle Crags to the north, drops to the road. Turn right and the car park is now 1.3km ahead on the left.

CENTRAL LAKES
Ambleside, Langdale, Grasmere and Thirlmere

Elter Water in summer with Lingmoor Fell behind (Walk 7)

Walk 7

Elterwater, Little Langdale and the waterfalls

*This walk starts in Great Langdale but quickly crosses to the gorgeous
neighbouring valley of Little Langdale, where it picks up a little-used
path along the base of Lingmoor Fell. With several ups and downs and
some rough ground underfoot, this is the only part of the whole route
that could be classed as anything but 'easy'. With stunning views across
Little Langdale Tarn towards Wetherlam and Swirl How, the bit of extra
effort is amply rewarded. Stony tracks and quiet lanes then lead east
towards the woods surrounding Colwith Force and Skelwith Force, two
impressive waterfalls. The easy stroll back into Elterwater, with its excellent
views of the Langdale Pikes, is a perfect way to end a perfect day.*

Start/finish	National Trust pay-and-display car park in Elterwater (NY 328 047)
Distance	11.4km (7 miles)
Total ascent	365m (1190ft)
Grade	2
Walking time	3¼hrs
Terrain	Good tracks; rough path along base of fells; quiet lanes; woodland trails
Maps	OS Explorer OL7; or OS Landranger 90
Refreshments	Britannia Inn, Elterwater
Transport	Bus 516

Leave the car park, turn left and walk along the road for about 300m. Then, as you draw level with the Eltermere Inn on the left, take the lane on the right – a cycle route to Coniston. Keep left at a fork – signposted Little Langdale.

The track rises gradually as it crosses into **Little Langdale**. Emerging from the trees and with the Coniston Fells providing a spectacular prospect ahead, you'll pass a path to Wilson Place on the left. About 200m after this, go through a small gate next to a larger gate on the right – set back slightly from the track.

A trail heads uphill, passing through two small gates as it does so. A few strides beyond the second of these, the path swings right and begins climbing more steeply. Leave it here by taking the less well-walked trail on the left. This soon follows the intake wall, which is your companion for the next 1.1km.

The vista across Little Langdale Tarn with the craggy slopes of Wetherlam and Swirl How rising dramatically behind it is captivating. There are many ups and downs as the path skirts the base of **Lingmoor Fell**. The top of one such rise affords the first uninterrupted view of the head of this beautiful valley.

Almost 1.1km beyond the last gate, the path drops into a small, wooded ravine. Don't be tempted by a faint path on the right; keep close to the wall. After negotiating a rock step, ford the small beck and go through the gate above. A narrow path runs beside the wall on the left for a while, but dissolves into the mire after about 200m. Now, simply keep to the high ground, staying reasonably close to the wall on the right and the way ahead will become clearer again.

Turn left when you reach the road and then go right at the T-junction. (A track on the right just before the junction cuts the corner.) About 300m after the junction, cross a bridge on your left and go through the gate to gain a track – signposted Tilberthwaite. After the cottage at Bridge End, the track climbs gently. Keep left at any forks and you'll eventually pass through a gate to find yourself on a walled route close to the old quarries.

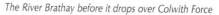

Watch for **Slater Bridge**, a popular beauty spot, down to the left after passing two sets of buildings. It is also possible to explore the disused quarry workings by crossing a stile beside a locked gate to the right of the main track about 150m beyond Slater Bridge. The stile provides access to a track that climbs to a short tunnel leading into the impressive cavern known as Cathedral Quarry.

Back on the main track, you reach a wooden footbridge across the River Brathay. Don't cross it; instead, turn right and then keep left as the track splits. Pass some buildings at **Stang End** and then reach a whitewashed farmhouse at High Park. Immediately after this, go through the kissing-gate next to the cattle grid on the left. Walk down the track towards the farmhouse, but then go

The River Brathay before it drops over Colwith Force

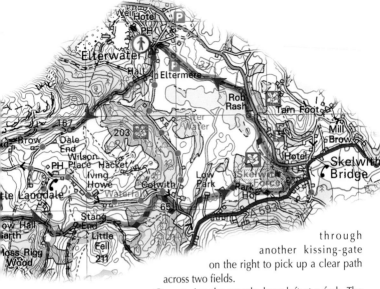

through
another kissing-gate
on the right to pick up a clear path
across two fields.

On entering the woods, bear left at a fork. The
path descends through the trees to the banks of the **River Brathay**. Two trails on
the left provide views of **Colwith Force**: the first takes you to the top of the falls;
the second, at the bottom of a pitched path, provides a more interesting perspective near the base of the white-water drop.

Beyond the falls, continue with the beck on your left. As you near a road
bridge, descend a rocky section and cross the stile to reach a minor road. Turn
right and, in about 100m, go through a tiny gated stile on the left – signposted
Skelwith Bridge. Follow the clear path over a couple of stiles and up to some
buildings. Cross the track here and continue on the path. At the next track, cross
diagonally left to pass beside the guesthouse. Go through the large wooden
gate to access a rough track between two walls. Follow this to the right at a
fingerpost.

On nearing the next set of buildings, including Park Cottage and Tiplog, go
through a pair of metal kissing-gates to join a track. About 130m beyond the cottages, take the surfaced path on the left. After entering the woods, ignore a path to
Skelwith Bridge on the right and continue downhill to cross a bridge over the River
Brathay. To visit the second waterfall on this route, **Skelwith Force**, turn right and
continue along the beck for about 80m. The main route, however, goes left after
the bridge.

Elter Water and Lingmoor Fell in winter

A well-constructed path now heads across riverside meadows, alongside the lake – **Elter Water** – and in and out of woodland, with some great views of the distinctive Langdale Pikes. It eventually follows **Great Langdale Beck** back to the Elterwater car park.

Walk 8

Great Langdale

Towered over by the iconic Langdale Pikes and culminating in the high wall of rock thrown up by the ridge comprising Crinkle Crags and Bow Fell, Great Langdale is one of the most dramatic of Lakeland valleys. Starting from Elterwater, this walk makes its way gradually up towards the valley head. It mostly uses tracks and paths in the valley bottom, but the first part of the day climbs up on to the low, grassy ridge of Dow Bank. The turning point on the walk is Mickleden Beck, crossed via a bridge.

The steep scree slopes of Pike o'Stickle

Start/finish	National Trust pay-and-display car park in Elterwater (NY 328 047)
Distance	15.6km (9¾ miles)
Total ascent	470m (1543ft)
Grade	2/3
Walking time	4½hrs
Terrain	Open, grassy fell; stony path across gill; valley tracks and paths; quiet lanes; one major ford
Maps	OS Explorer OL6 and OL7; or OS Landranger 90
Refreshments	Britannia Inn and Elterwater Café in Elterwater; Old Dungeon Ghyll, New Dungeon Ghyll and Sticklebarn in Great Langdale
Transport	Bus 516

From the car park entrance, turn right and then, as you pass the Britannia Inn, take the road on the left. Go straight across when you reach the main road through

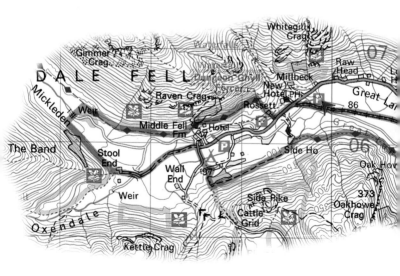

Descending into Great Langdale after crossing Megs Gill

Langdale. Follow the minor road up towards a pretty white cottage and then round to the right, soon passing a small building on your left.

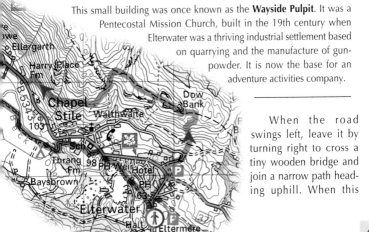

This small building was once known as the **Wayside Pulpit**. It was a Pentecostal Mission Church, built in the 19th century when Elterwater was a thriving industrial settlement based on quarrying and the manufacture of gunpowder. It is now the base for an adventure activities company.

When the road swings left, leave it by turning right to cross a tiny wooden bridge and join a narrow path heading uphill. When this

The Langdale Pikes in winter

regains the road, cross diagonally left to continue on the path. About 90m up from the road, turn left to cross a flat area and pick up a path that soon begins climbing steeply. As you make your way steadily up the grassy slope, keep right at any forks. As soon as you reach the ridge and get your first glimpse of the fells to the north-east, including Fairfield, you hit a crossing of paths. Turn left here, soon climbing again to reach the cairn-topped summit of **Dow Bank** (280m) and its magnificent view of the Langdale Pikes.

Continue along this lovely section of low, grassy ridge in a generally north-west direction, keeping either to the main path or the one just above it along the top of the high ground. (Avoid straying on to any of the paths heading right.) On reaching a large cairn at a junction of paths at the base of more rugged looking terrain, turn sharp left.

Walk steeply downhill on grass at first, but then swing right along a narrow, rocky path that clings to the side of the steep ravine. The path is very loose and there are steep drops to the left, so watch your footing. It leads to a rocky area at the top of the Megs Gill waterfall. After crossing this, head steeply downhill with the gill to your left. When the path splits, bear right. At the next faint fork, keep right again to follow a dramatic, balcony path about 110m above the slate-built village of **Chapel Stile**.

The reappearance of the **Langdale Pikes** is a moment that's likely to stop you in your tracks. Up until now, these distinctive fells have been distant objects only partially seen, but here they are, in their full glory, rising relentlessly from the green valley bottom.

After passing a prominent crag on the left, the path descends more steeply. You soon have a drystone wall on your left and, when this swings sharp left, the path appears to end. Turn left to descend the steep, grassy hillside. Head towards the small gate in a fence at the bottom of the slope and, once through, keep close to the wall on your right to descend to the road.

A 200m detour along the road to the left brings you to Copt Howe, a **prehistoric rock art site**. Rediscovered in 1999, the large boulders, which can be visited via a gate in the wall to the right of the road, boast a series of cup-and-ring markings believed to have been created between 4000 and 6000 years ago.

Turn right and walk along the asphalt for 300m. Turn left along a broad track – signposted Dungeon Ghyll. (There is a small layby with a postbox in it close to the start of the track.) Even closer now, the crags and peaks of the Langdale Pikes tower imperiously over their valley, Harrison Stickle taking centre stage.

The track ends at the National Park Authority's Langdale car park. Cross this and turn left along the main valley road, but then take the turning on the right into the National Trust's Stickle Ghyll car park. You'll see a path signposted to the Old Dungeon Ghyll on your left. Next to this is a lump of smooth rock. Head to the right of this rock and cross the stile in the fence ahead. As you head uphill, don't be tempted by the gap in the wall on your left just beyond the trees; simply keep on beside the wall.

Go through the small gate at the top of the enclosure and turn left. Fork left immediately after the kissing-gate, soon passing beneath some popular climbing crags as you continue your journey towards the valley head. After going through a kissing-gate above the buildings of the Old Dungeon Ghyll, the path drops to a clearer track, along which you turn right.

The **National Trust** owns much of Great Langdale, not just the high ground but also two of the valley's pubs, a campsite and several farms. The Trust's relationship with Langdale dates back to 1929 when the wealthy historian George Macaulay Trevelyan gifted the Old Dungeon Ghyll Hotel and 20 hectares of adjoining land to the conservation charity. It was the Trust's first property in the valley. Later, Trevelyan also bought Stool End Farm, Wall End Farm, Mill Beck Farm and Harry Place Farm, all of which were eventually donated to the National Trust.

The track now heads up into wild **Mickleden**, past a series of walled valley enclosures and with magnificent fell scenery closing in around you. About 1.4km beyond the Old Dungeon Ghyll, you lose the wall on your left. Strike off left here

Looking up Mickleden towards Bow Fell and Rossett Gill

to make your way across pathless ground to Mickleden Beck, about 120m southwest of the track.

Cross the bridge and walk downstream beside the beck for a few strides. A stony trail then climbs the embankment. When it vanishes, continue in the same direction to reach a broad track. Bear left along this and then bear right at a fork close to a gate with a 'private' sign on it.

The steep, scree-covered slopes on the other side of Mickleden Beck belong to **Pike o'Stickle**, one of the Langdale Pikes and home to a Neolithic 'axe factory'. Here, high up on the exposed fellside, Stone Age people once quarried an exposed seam of greenstone and roughed out axe heads from it. The end result must have been quite impressive because there was a significant trade in these tools, Langdale axes having been found as far away as Cornwall.

On reaching the buildings at **Stool End**, go left through the gate. Follow the signs down into the farmyard and round to the right to leave via a sealed track. On reaching the road, turn right. When it swings sharp right, go through the gate on the left into the National Trust's campsite – signposted Blea Tarn. Continue straight ahead for about 50m. A footpath marker directs you right, over a small wooden bridge. Climb gently uphill, through two kissing-gates and then through a gap in a wall. Bear half-right to a gate into a small plantation. Leave the trees via a gate and turn sharp left.

The faint path goes through a gate, continuing parallel with the fence on your left. From the fence corner, descend slightly across some boggy ground and then keep right, on a clearer, narrow path, which contours the hillside to a ladder stile. Cross this and then, after a second stile followed immediately by a small bridge above **Side House**, continue in the same direction (north-east) for about 60m. Straight after crossing another small beck, bear left to head towards the buildings. Don't cross the bridge; instead turn right along the clear path.

After the next kissing-gate, the path climbs, but then drops back to the valley bottom again. Soon after a gate, walkers are funnelled between old walls. Follow the path around a sharp bend to the right and as far as an old barn. Bear left at this junction – signposted Great Langdale. The path quickly swings left to pass in front of a cottage called **Oak Howe**.

Don't be tempted by the first bridge over **Great Langdale Beck**; just keep following the clear, wide track downstream. It later crosses a humpback bridge and

Bow Fell from Great Langdale

then swings right. When it then swings left near the road in Chapel Stile, leave it by turning right along a path. As you reach the buildings, follow the sealed lane left. Then, making sure you don't head up to the farm buildings, turn right at the next track junction to walk with the school's wall on your left. Keep the wall on your left until you reach the road.

Turn right to walk along the asphalt and, soon after passing the Wainwrights' Inn, turn right to cross Great Langdale Beck via a footbridge – signposted Little Langdale. Once on the other side, turn left. Eventually, you reach a lane, along which you bear left. Turn left at the T-junction to return to the car park, which is a few metres ahead on the right.

Walk 9
Circuit of Loughrigg Fell

Apart from one or two short climbs, this wonderful circuit of Loughrigg Fell makes for a fairly gentle outing. Always on clear, easy-to-follow paths, the spectacular views change with every twist and turn on the walk. Fairfield and Windermere look impressive early on, but the best is yet to come…The Langdale Pikes, first glimpsed in all their splendour as you round Ivy Crag, later provide a magnificent backdrop to beautiful Loughrigg Tarn. And, as if that wasn't enough, the return route on the northern side of the fell passes high above the serene lakes of Grasmere and Rydal Water on a superb terrace path complete with several well-placed benches from which to enjoy the view.

Enjoying a break beside Loughrigg Tarn

Start/finish	Rydal Road car park in Ambleside, just N of village centre on A591 (NY 374 047)
Distance	11km (7 miles)
Total ascent	415m (1362ft)
Grade	2
Walking time	3¼hrs
Terrain	Quiet lanes; tracks
Maps	OS Explorer OL7; or OS Landranger 90
Refreshments	Choice of pubs, cafés and restaurants in Ambleside
Transport	Ambleside is well served by buses. There are regular services between the town and Carlisle, Keswick, Grasmere, Great Langdale, Hawkshead, Coniston, Windermere, Newby Bridge, Kendal, Barrow-in-Furness and Lancaster

Using the pedestrian bridge, leave the car park and turn right along the road. Keep right when the road forks. Just after the cinema, turn right and immediately left. Pass St Mary's Parish Church on your left and then walk straight across the park. Cross one bridge and then go over the humpback bridge over the **River Rothay**. Turn right along the quiet lane and then, about 50m beyond the cattle grid, turn left to ascend a surfaced track.

This heads uphill fairly steeply at first, but the gradient eases soon after passing a small group of homes. Keep to the surfaced lane, which soon goes over to gravel. After a couple of gates, you find yourself on open land. Continue ahead on the same stony track and, at a gap in the wall on your right, you can see across to the Fairfield Horseshoe.

After another gate, the views west begin to open out – with Wetherlam appearing

Looking down on Grasmere from Loughrigg Terrace

straight ahead. The constructed path descends to a small stream, which can be crossed by stepping stones when the water level is high. Immediately after crossing, ignore the path to the right; keep to the clear track. There is a lovely view of Windermere to your left here.

The path now descends, soon running beside a drystone wall on the left. The bracken-covered slopes to your right belong to Loughrigg Fell. When the path splits, take the left branch down to a tall gate from where you can see Skelwith Bridge. Do not go through the gate; instead, keep right to stay with the level path around the base of the fell.

Later go through a gate with a sign on the drystone wall reading 'Elterwater and Langdale'. Head downhill on the loose, stony track for a further 200m. You'll now see two gates close to each other on the right. Go through the second one. (It has a footpath and 'no cycling' sign on it.) Walking to the left of a group of beech trees, cross the small field and climb the stile at the other side. Walk briefly with the fence on your right before the faint path heads downhill towards **Loughrigg Tarn**. Cross the stile and turn right along the gravel lane.

The tiny **Loughrigg Tarn**, sitting at an altitude of less than 100m, occupies an idyllic location that has the Langdale Pikes as its immaculate backdrop. Wordsworth described it as a 'most beautiful example' and gave it its nickname 'Diana's looking glass' after the Italian Lake Nemi, said to be the mirror of Diana, the Roman warrior goddess of nature and fertility.

Walkers making their way towards Loughrigg Tarn

On reaching a road, go through the gate and turn right. Walk along the asphalt for about 400m. Ignore one path to the left early on, but then turn left through a second wooden gate into a small area of attractive woodland known as High Close Garden. The gravel path soon splits; bear right here along the narrower branch to walk gently uphill. Turn right at the top to climb some steps and leave the woodland via a gate.

Turn left along the road and then go through the gate on your right into Deerbolts Wood – signposted Loughrigg Terrace and Rydal. This clear, wide track is soon joined by another as it drops to a metal kissing-gate, which provides access to open land again.

Ignoring the path heading steeply uphill on your right, walk along **Loughrigg Terrace**, high above the wooded shores of Grasmere and with spectacular views towards the pass at Dunmail Raise. There are plenty of opportunities to sit and admire the scenery on one of the many benches along this stretch of the walk.

Take the next clear path on your right, where a public bridleway marker indicates that the main path goes left. This heads gently uphill at first and then drops to a junction with a wider track. Bear right here. The lake down to your left now is Rydal Water. The track makes its way to the higher of the Rydal Caves and then winds its way down to the lower cave. Both caves are manmade, a result of slate quarrying.

Keep to the wide track, going through a gate just after joining another path from the left. The route eventually goes over to asphalt and drops to a T-junction. Turn right and follow the road as it winds its way towards Ambleside, beside the **River Rothay**. After almost 1.9km, you reach the cattle grid you crossed earlier in the walk.

Cross the humpback bridge on the left. You could now retrace your steps to the car park via the park. Alternatively, immediately after crossing the bridge, go through the metal gate and follow the surfaced path to a residential street. Turn left along this and then right at the main road to return to the car park.

THE ROMANTICS AND EARLY TOURISM

Easedale Tarn

The Lake District hasn't always been the magnet for tourists that it is today. Before the second half of the 18th century, it was regarded as an inhospitable place, bounded by hostile mountains. Writing in 1724, Daniel Defoe described the Westmorland landscape as 'the wildest, most barren and frightful of any that I have passed over in England, or even Wales itself'.

It was only later in the century, after the improvement of the turnpike roads, that more travellers braved these wild regions and began to see the mountains in a more favourable light. Father Thomas West's 1778 *A Guide to the Lakes*, full of praise and purple prose, was probably the first real guidebook, intended to help would-be visitors. At the same time, the Cumberland-born priest and artist William Gilpin was putting forward his 'principles of picturesque beauty'. Unusual at the time, he looked at the natural world and saw something aesthetically pleasing.

This appreciation of the Lake District's natural beauty was also the inspiration for the Romantic poets. Throughout the late 18th and early 19th centuries Wordsworth, Coleridge, Southey and others were waxing lyrical about the waterfalls, the tarns, even the daffodils. Along with great landscape painters such as Turner, they were clearly moved by what they saw, and helped put the Lake District, including places such as Loughrigg Tarn and Easedale Tarn, on the map. This coincided with the birth of the railways, giving tourism a massive boost, as travel ceased to be the preserve of the wealthiest.

Walk 10

Orrest Head and Wansfell Pike

There's something very special about linear walks: that sense of satisfaction you get from completing a journey from one place to another on foot is hard to beat. This one links Windermere with Ambleside via Orrest Head, Troutbeck and, the highest point on the walk, Wansfell Pike (482m). It's a lovely walk with views that are constantly changing: one minute you're gazing out across the lake, the next you're staring up into the wilds of the Kentmere Fells or across to the Langdale Pikes.

The western arm of the Kentmere Horseshoe seen from the climb to Wansfell Pike

Start	Windermere railway station (SD 413 986)
Finish	Kelsick Road, Ambleside (NY 376 042)
Distance	12.9km (8 miles)
Total ascent	590m (1930ft)
Grade	4
Walking time	4hrs
Terrain	Tracks; field paths; quiet lanes; open felltop with steep descent; woodland trail
Maps	OS Explorer OL7; or OS Landrangers 97 and 90
Refreshments	Choice of pubs, cafés and restaurants in Windermere and Ambleside; Mortal Man Inn in Troutbeck
Transport	Windermere is connected by rail to Kendal and Oxenholme; bus services 505, 555 and 599 link Windermere with Ambleside

With your back to Windermere railway station, turn left along the access road and then, at the complicated junction where the station driveway meets the **A591**, carefully cross to the north side of the main road. Turn left along the A591 for a few metres until you see a lane heading up to the right, clearly signposted to Orrest Head. Follow this, ignoring a path to the left early on.

The lane winds gently uphill through the trees. On reaching a bench close to the entrance to the blacksmith's yard, bear right at a fork. Swinging right, you reach a wall. Turn right here and then go through what remains of an old metal gate on your left to gain the steps that lead to the summit of **Orrest Head**.

On Orrest Head

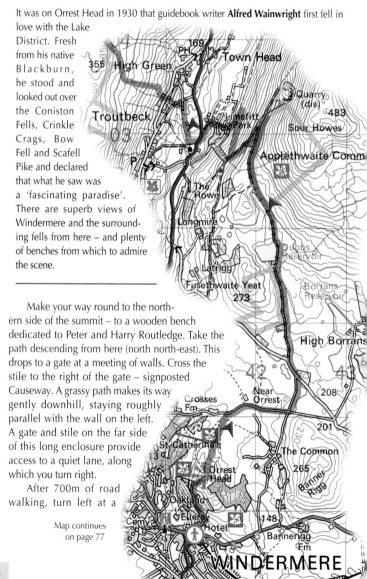

It was on Orrest Head in 1930 that guidebook writer **Alfred Wainwright** first fell in love with the Lake District. Fresh from his native Blackburn, he stood and looked out over the Coniston Fells, Crinkle Crags, Bow Fell and Scafell Pike and declared that what he saw was a 'fascinating paradise'. There are superb views of Windermere and the surrounding fells from here – and plenty of benches from which to admire the scene.

Make your way round to the northern side of the summit – to a wooden bench dedicated to Peter and Harry Routledge. Take the path descending from here (north north-east). This drops to a gate at a meeting of walls. Cross the stile to the right of the gate – signposted Causeway. A grassy path makes its way gently downhill, staying roughly parallel with the wall on the left. A gate and stile on the far side of this long enclosure provide access to a quiet lane, along which you turn right.

After 700m of road walking, turn left at a

Map continues
on page 77

Dubbs Road

crossroads. Go left again at a T-junction – along Moorhowe Road. About 200m along this road, take the broad track on the right, known as Dubbs Road. This lovely old byway takes you past **Dubbs Reservoir** and up to a high point of 279m. Eventually, you are able to look down on idyllic Troutbeck, where drystone walls snake up and down the hillsides.

Dubbs Reservoir was originally constructed to supply Windermere, but then became an adjunct to the Thirlmere Aqueduct, serving Manchester. The reservoir and beck downstream provide important habitats for rare pearl mussels and native white-clawed crayfish.

On reaching a junction with another track – the Garburn Road – go sharp left, turning your back on the lovely fell scenery that has just appeared. After almost 600m along this track, take the narrower track on the right, quickly going through a gate. With views up to the head of the valley, this track eases its way down to a tall gate. Turn sharp left just before the gate.

The path emerges behind the Haybarn Inn, part of **Limefitt** holiday park. Turn right to descend the steps and then keep straight ahead on the driveway through

Ridge wall on Wansfell

the middle of the site. Having passed the barrier on the far side of the bridge over Trout Beck, bear left along Limefitt's wide driveway.

At the top, turn left and walk along the main road for just 100m. There is a small layby on the right. Just above this, hidden by the vegetation, is a finger-post and wall stile. Climb this and walk straight across the small enclosure to a second stile. Continue in the same direction – with a children's play area down to the left – to a small gate. Go through this and then through a larger gate on the right.

A grassy path heads gently uphill, beside a fence at first. It later becomes fenced on both sides and then broadens. On reaching a junction of tracks at a fingerpost, turn left. In another 90m, turn right along a bridleway. Follow this to the road in Troutbeck and then turn left. Almost immediately, turn right along a track and through a gate – signposted Wansfell Pike and Ambleside.

This track, known as Nanny Lane, climbs steadily between drystone walls above Troutbeck. Almost 1.2km after leaving the village, the stony track goes over to grass. Turn left through the metal gate here. A well-trodden path ascends the east slopes of **Wansfell**, steepening in its later stages.

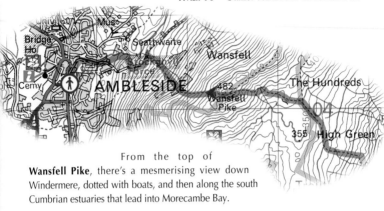

From the top of
Wansfell Pike, there's a mesmerising view down
Windermere, dotted with boats, and then along the south
Cumbrian estuaries that lead into Morecambe Bay.

Go through the small gate in the ridge fence. The way down isn't obvious at
first. There are a couple of paths leading away from the summit rocks over to the
left. Both of them drop on to an obvious path on the north-west side of the fell.
This winds its way painstakingly in the general direction of Ambleside.

Crossing a bridge and going through a kissing-gate along the way, continue
downhill to reach a lane. Turn left along the asphalt. Then, about 90m after a cattle grid, take the fenced path on the right. This goes through a gate next to an old
metal turnstile and heads into the woods. On reaching the railings beside **Stock
Ghyll**, turn left. As you head downhill, a series of viewing platforms on the right
allow safe glimpses of the dramatic waterfalls of **Stockghyll Force** and the attractive, steep-sided ravine through which they tumble.

Keep left at any path junctions to re-emerge on the lane you were following
a short while ago. Bear right, and it drops you on to Market Place in Ambleside.
Turn left and then take the second road on the right – Kelsick Road. The bus stop
for Windermere is a few metres ahead on the right.

Walk 11

Grasmere and Rydal Water

In and out of pretty woodland, beside sparkling lakes and with majestic fell scenery all around, this walk explores the heart of Wordsworth country, the area that inspired one of England's greatest poets. It follows quiet lanes and pleasant tracks from Wordsworth's burial place in Grasmere and past two of his homes to the tiny village of Rydal. It then returns along the shores of two small, but beautiful lakes, Rydal Water and Grasmere.

Seat Sandal towers over Grasmere

Start/finish	The parish church of St Oswald's in Grasmere village (NY 337 073)
Distance	9.4km (6 miles)
Total ascent	245m (805ft)
Grade	1
Walking time	2½hrs
Terrain	Woodland and lakeside paths; quiet country lanes
Maps	OS Explorer OL7; or OS Landranger 90
Refreshments	Choice of cafés, bars and restaurants in Grasmere; Badger Bar in Rydal
Transport	Buses 555, 555R and 599

The walk starts from **St Oswald's Church**, where William Wordsworth and members of his family are buried. With your back to the church, turn left along the road. On reaching the roundabout on the **A591**, turn right towards Ambleside and immediately left. Watch for two interesting features along this lane: Dove Cottage and, slightly further on, a flat-topped boulder on the left, known as the Coffin Stone.

Dove Cottage was the home of William Wordsworth and his sister Dorothy from 1799 until 1808. The building has been open to visitors since 1899 and still houses much of the Wordsworths' original furniture. It also contains a set of scales which is said to have been used by William's young friend, Thomas de Quincey to weigh

his opium. De Quincey, probably best known for his 1821 work *Confessions of an English Opium-Eater*, moved into the cottage after the Wordsworths moved out, soon upsetting them by making alterations to their beloved garden.

Dove Cottage

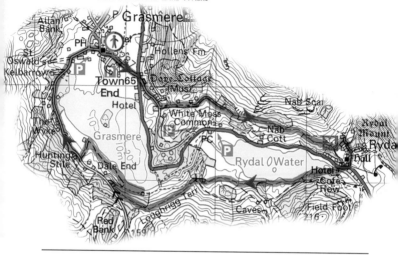

This lane and the track you follow as far as Rydal used to be known as the **Corpse Road**. Before St Mary's Church in Ambleside was consecrated, coffins had to be transported along this route from Ambleside to St Oswald's Church in Grasmere for interment. The Coffin Stone was used to support the coffin while the bearers rested.

RYDAL MOUNT

Rydal Mount was Wordsworth's home from 1813 until he died in 1850. Like all his homes, this one was only rented – it belonged to the Le Flemings of Rydal Hall. Wordsworth did, however, own a patch of ground behind the church and had intended to build a home for his daughter Dora on it. After she died in 1847, he planted hundreds of daffodils there in her memory. The site, Dora's Field, is now in the care of the National Trust.

The entrance to Rydal Hall is passed further down the lane. This building dates from the 17th century, although the front is Victorian. The hall and grounds now form part of a conference centre and retreat run by the Diocese of Carlisle. In 2005, work began on restoring the Italianate terraced gardens designed by landscape architect Thomas Mawson; it was completed two years later.

On the path above Rydal Water

Take the second lane on the left – signposted 'Alcock Tarn and Coffin Route to Rydal'. The surfaced lane narrows and becomes rougher after Dunnabeck, the last of a group of cottages. It narrows further as it passes to the right of a solitary cottage called Brockstone. Keep left when a path heads right soon after this building. Follow the path in and out of pretty woodland and across grazing land with views down to Rydal Water and across to Loughrigg Fell. The path forks on a couple of occasions, but it doesn't matter which branch you take. You eventually come out on a quiet lane at Rydal. Turn right, quickly passing **Rydal Mount**.

On reaching the busy A591, carefully cross over and turn right. As you draw level with the Badger Bar, go through the gap in the wall on your left. After crossing the footbridge over the **River Rothay**, turn right. The river soon becomes **Rydal Water**. Keep close to the water's edge for as long as possible, but as you pass Heron Island, a drystone wall forces you uphill, away from the lake. Ignoring paths on the left to Rydal Caves, climb to a rise that allows you your first glimpse of Grasmere below. Bear left along the level path, known as **Loughrigg Terrace**, which provides excellent views of the lake.

The terrace path ends at a gate on the edge of the woods. Go through this and immediately turn right, through a wooden gate, to enter Deerbolts Wood. After descending to a slate cottage, take the narrow path on the right – signposted Grasmere Lake. Turn left on reaching a clear path close to the lake. With views

A summer's evening beside Grasmere

across to Seat Sandal, Stone Arthur and Heron Pike, this lovely shore route continues beyond the woods. Sadly, after less than 1km, it swings away the water's edge and climbs to a lane.

Turn right and walk along the asphalt for 1.5km. Re-entering the village of Grasmere, keep right – towards Ambleside – to reach a T-junction opposite the church where the walk started.

Walk 12

Easedale Tarn and Tarn Crag

Tarn Crag (549m) is not on any list of classic Lakeland fells and so is often bypassed by all but a few peak-baggers keen to tick off the Wainwrights. However, its wonderful ridge offers superb views across to the Helvellyn and Fairfield ranges as well as a chance to have the fells all to yourself – a rare treat indeed! On the way from Grasmere, the route passes the impressive waterfalls of Sour Milk Gill, gorgeous Easedale Tarn and peaceful Codale Tarn. Beyond the final tarn, the clear paths disappear and the feeling of adventure begins.

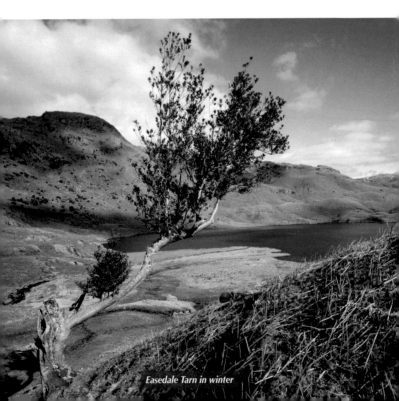

Easedale Tarn in winter

Start/finish	Grasmere village at the beginning of Easedale Road, opposite Sam Read's bookshop (NY 337 076)
Distance	11km (7 miles)
Total ascent	540m (1770ft)
Grade	5
Walking time	4hrs
Terrain	Good paths in Easedale and Far Easedale; short rocky section; pathless open fell
Maps	OS Explorers OL6 and OL7; or OS Landranger 90
Refreshments	Choice of cafés, bars and restaurants in Grasmere
Transport	Buses 555, 555R and 599

From the village centre, head north-west along Easedale Road for 900m. As the road bends sharp right, you'll see a small footbridge in some trees to the left – signposted Easedale Tarn. Cross this and then a second, smaller bridge.

Stick to the clear, beckside track until it goes through a gate. After this, go straight over the farm track – crossing a bridge over a beck in the process. After the next gate, the rough path, pitched in places, climbs beside the powerful waterfalls of **Sour Milk Gill**. The gradient then eases briefly at the top of the falls before one final pull to reach **Easedale Tarn**.

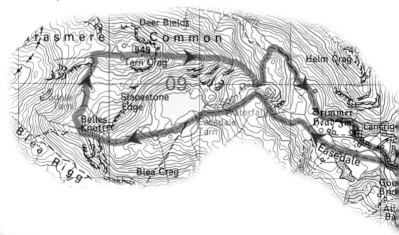

A bird's eye view of Codale Tarn

Easedale Tarn has been a popular destination for walkers for many years. In Victorian times, there was even a refreshment hut up here – almost 300m above sea level – and a small boat was available for hire on the tarn.

Follow the main path as it skirts the south side of the tarn and then climbs into wilder, less visited country. The path is steep in places and you'll need your hands for balance as you clamber up the bare rock just below **Belles Knott**.

Having left the rocky sections behind, the gradient suddenly eases and the ground ahead opens out. Leave the main path here by turning right along a narrow path that quickly drops to cross the beck. The path skirts the edge of lovely **Codale Tarn**. Cross the outlet stream and continue to the north end of the tarn where the stony path ends.

Just before the inlet stream, you reach a faint, grassy fork in the path. Bear right (north-east) here. You'll have to leap across the inlet stream on a couple of occasions as you climb away from the tarn. Drawing level with a sheepfold to the left, you begin to climb more steeply, now heading mainly north. As you ascend the zig-zagging path, make sure that, on reaching the base of a small crag, you don't miss the final bend to the right (north-east).

On the ridge proper, with its grand view across to the Helvellyn range, turn right. There's some boggy ground here, so the path isn't obvious at first: simply head south-east and you'll soon see a grassy trail winding its way east. Just before the path starts dropping steeply, it forks. The main route is to the right, but a detour to the left takes you to the highest point of **Tarn Crag**, a wonderful viewpoint where walkers will no doubt want to linger on a clear day.

Continuing on the main route, head steeply down the shallow, grassy gully cutting between the crags. A faint line of zig-zags eases the descent. At the bottom of this first drop, keep heading east along the faint, grassy ridge path; don't be tempted by clearer paths to the right – although the worst that could happen would be that you'd end up back at Easedale Tarn. There are no right and wrong ways of descending this lonely ridge. There are faint paths all over the place – some stick to the highest ground, some don't. Making sure you head generally east and never stray too far from the ridge, choose the options that suit you best – and enjoy!

In the lower stages, the ridge path descends through bracken and swings south-east. Nearing the becks above the Sour Milk Gill falls, it forks. Take either branch and, within a few metres, reach a T-junction. Turn left here. You're unlikely to go wrong now – the path is clear and there are yellow waymarkers to guide you. Make sure you swing left on nearing a drystone wall.

Approaching the valley bottom, veer right where a path joins from the left. Cross the footbridge in **Far Easedale** and turn right to head downstream. You eventually lose the beck, but the way ahead is obvious. At a junction of tracks, keep straight ahead – signposted Grasmere. Go through the gate and head down the lane. On reaching a road, turn left and walk back to the village.

Walk 13
Thirlmere circuit

Although not a natural lake, Thirlmere occupies an atmospheric spot between the mountains of the Helvellyn range to the east and low-lying, heather-clad fells to the west. This circuit of the reservoir is extremely varied, making use of a series of permissive paths that weave in and out of the woodland along the western shore as well as forest paths on Helvellyn's western slopes. Leaving the trees at Swirls, the route ends with a walk along a superb path just above the intake wall.

The Helvellyn range from the northern end of the reservoir

Start/finish	Thirlmere Recreation Hall, Legburthwaite – close to the junction of the B5322 and A591 (NY 318 189)
Distance	16.6km (10¼ miles)
Total ascent	485m (1590ft)
Grade	2/3
Walking time	5¼hrs
Terrain	Quiet roads; lakeside trail; forest tracks and paths; rough path at base of fells; risk of flooding
Maps	OS Explorers OL5; or OS Landranger 90
Refreshments	King's Head, Thirlspot
Transport	Bus 555
Note	After heavy rain, some sections along the W shore of Thirlmere may be under water, and walkers will need to divert on to the quiet road running parallel with the path

From the entrance to the Recreation Hall's car park, turn left along the **B5322** and then go right at the T-junction to walk along the grass verge of the **A591**. Take the next road on the left, later crossing the dam over the northern end of **Thirlmere**.

Thirlmere reservoir was formed in 1894 by damming two small, natural lakes. Victorian engineers devised a system, still in use today, which allows water to flow by gravity, without any pumps, all the way from the reservoir to Manchester, 160km away. The water takes just over a day to reach the city.

Go through a small gate on the left just before the next road junction. Follow the path south along the water's edge, turn left when it comes back on to the asphalt for a short while and then regain the shore path via the next gate. As you follow the shore path, look across the water to the Helvellyn range, its steep slopes slashed by silver lines as foaming becks come crashing down from the heights. The second half of the walk traverses these slopes, providing a more intimate view of the dramatic watercourses.

The path passes through the **Armboth** car park and continues south, in and out of woodland. Keep left at any forks, staying with the path closest to the

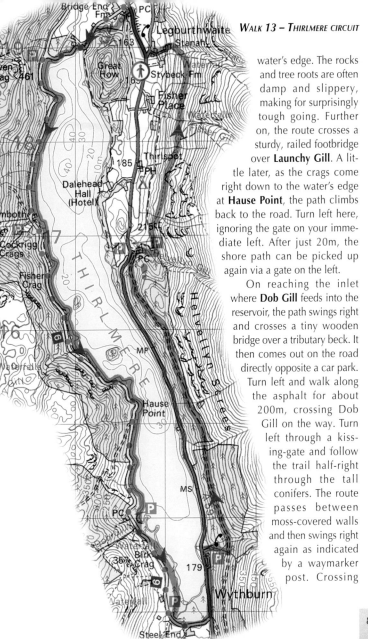

water's edge. The rocks and tree roots are often damp and slippery, making for surprisingly tough going. Further on, the route crosses a sturdy, railed footbridge over **Launchy Gill**. A little later, as the crags come right down to the water's edge at **Hause Point**, the path climbs back to the road. Turn left here, ignoring the gate on your immediate left. After just 20m, the shore path can be picked up again via a gate on the left.

On reaching the inlet where **Dob Gill** feeds into the reservoir, the path swings right and crosses a tiny wooden bridge over a tributary beck. It then comes out on the road directly opposite a car park. Turn left and walk along the asphalt for about 200m, crossing Dob Gill on the way. Turn left through a kissing-gate and follow the trail half-right through the tall conifers. The route passes between moss-covered walls and then swings right again as indicated by a waymarker post. Crossing

The Helvellyn range from the southern end of Thirlmere

several stretches of boardwalk, the trail winds its way through the trees. Keep right at a fork marked by a waymarker post.

The permissive shore path finally ends at the **Steel End** car park. Turn left along the road. On reaching the junction with the A591, carefully cross over and turn left – over a plank bridge and through two gates in quick succession – to gain a path running parallel with the road. Turn right along **Wythburn** church's access lane. As you pass the church, cross the car park and go through the gate in the far wall, ignoring the gate down to the left. Turn right, through a tall gate, to head steeply uphill through tall conifers beside Comb Gill.

On reaching a clear forest track, turn left – signposted Swirls. About 1.1km after joining this track, you reach a more open area and a fork in the path. Bear right: through a gate, over two bridges and then through a second gate. Compared with the straightforward track lower down the slope, this narrow path provides a more atmospheric experience of the woods that cling to Helvellyn's lower slopes. Eventually though, it drops back on to the track and you simply continue in the same direction until you reach the northern edge of the forest.

After leaving the trees, go through the small gate on the right and turn right to enter the Swirls car park. Cross the bridge at the far end of the main parking area

View from Thirlmere Dam

– signposted Helvellyn, Stanah, Sticks Pass. The path follows the beck upstream for a short while. At a faint fork, bear left along the clearer route. This climbs through another gate and crosses a small bridge. Just before the next bridge, turn left, aiming for a gate next to a wall corner.

Once through this, you are on a reasonably clear path just above the intake wall, with views of Skiddaw and Blencathra ahead. Keep right at a waymarker – along the higher, clearer path. The route briefly becomes unclear after crossing a bridge; simply keep close to the wall on the left as it climbs.

Keep straight on at the next fingerpost and then left at a fork, staying with the well-used path. After crossing a gated bridge over dramatic **Fisher Gill**, the path goes through a gate and then cuts straight across the open hillside, briefly losing sight of the wall. Dropping to a fingerpost close to **Stanah Gill**, don't be tempted by the small gate in the wall; instead, go through the gate in the fence to cross the

FROM LAKES TO RESERVOIRS

Manchester Corporation plaque on Thirlmere Dam

With its popula-
tion growing and
industry putting
increasing pres-
sure on water sup-
plies, Manchester
began to turn its
thirsty eyes to the Lake District in the late 19th century. The Manchester
Corporation first looked at Windermere and Ullswater, but then turned
its attention to the Thirlmere area. Despite being stalled by the Thirlmere
Defence Association, the reservoir eventually received Royal Assent in 1879
and Manchester was granted the right to extract 25 gallons of water per head
per day. The first water to arrive in the city from Thirlmere was marked with
an official ceremony on 13 October 1894.

The next major reservoir project was the creation of Haweswater in the
Eastern Lake District. An Act of Parliament in 1919 gave the go-ahead to build
the dam that would drown Mardale and produce the enormous reservoir. The
inhabitants of two villages and scattered farmsteads had to be moved and 100
bodies buried in Holy Trinity churchyard were exhumed and reburied in Shap
before the valley was flooded in 1935. Even today, almost 80 years later, the
walls of the village of Mardale Green reappear in times of drought.

Although United Utilities water company draws small amounts of water
from other lakes in the National Park, attempts to convert any into full-blown
reservoirs have been resisted. For example, in the early 1960s, Manchester
began to eye up Ullswater again. The Ulverston-born barrister and MP Lord
William Norman Birkett successfully led a parliamentary campaign to defeat
Manchester's plans.

beck. After the next gate, head down the hillside and through another gate. After
the ladder stile at the bottom of the slope, turn left along the lane. The car park
where the walk started is now about 200m ahead on your left.

WESTERN VALLEYS
Eskdale, Wasdale and Buttermere area

Stanley Ghyll (Walk 14)

Walk 14

Stanley Ghyll Force and River Esk

This mostly gentle stroll visits some of the highlights of the middle section of beautiful Eskdale. After a riverside saunter and a walk along an excellent bridleway that weaves its way in and out of delightful woodland, the route heads up into the lush ravine of Stanley Ghyll. Here, at the head of the gorge, is one of the Lake District's most stunning waterfalls.

Doctor Bridge over the River Esk

Start/finish	Pay-and-display car park at Dalegarth Station, near Boot, Eskdale (NY 173 007)
Distance	7km (4½ miles)
Total ascent	170m (550ft)
Grade	1
Walking time	2¼hrs
Terrain	Quiet lanes; woodland and riverside paths; slippery rocks in gorge can be avoided
Maps	OS Explorer OL6; or OS Landrangers 89 and 96
Refreshments	Boot Inn and Brook House Inn in Boot; Fellbites Café at Dalegarth Station
Transport	Dalegarth Station is served by the Ravenglass and Eskdale Railway (01229 717171 www.ravenglass-railway.co.uk)

From the entrance to Dalegarth Station, turn left along the road. On reaching the Brook House Inn, turn right along a wide track – signposted St Catherine's Church. Keep right at the fork. On reaching the church, turn left along the riverside path – signposted Doctor Bridge.

Soon after the next gate, you'll see two paths running parallel with each other. The lower one is the route of the old railway that served the iron mines on the southern side of the valley, but our route uses the higher path. (A 200m detour up the disused railway leads to a picturesque little gorge where the railway crossed the river via a girder bridge.)

Continue upstream on the northern side of the **River Esk** until you reach the humpback stone bridge known as Doctor Bridge. Cross this and immediately

St Catherine's Church, Eskdale

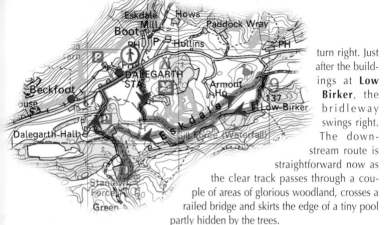

turn right. Just after the buildings at **Low Birker**, the bridleway swings right. The downstream route is straightforward now as the clear track passes through a couple of areas of glorious woodland, crosses a railed bridge and skirts the edge of a tiny pool partly hidden by the trees.

Almost 1.5km beyond Low Birker, the path becomes softer underfoot as it passes through an area of bracken. You have a low wall on your right at first. When this ends, swing right and then left on a broad, grassy swathe through the bracken. After the next gate, cross the railed footbridge over the beck issuing from Stanley Ghyll. Another gate leads into a small field. Cross this and go through the gate on the other side to reach a stony track. Turn left here to begin the second loop of the walk. (You'll return to this crossing of ways after visiting Stanley Ghyll Force.)

Just as the track swings right and before it starts to climb, go through the small gate on your left, signposted to the waterfalls. A clear path heads upstream through a beautiful area of mixed woodland. Native species, which are actively encouraged, include sessile oak, birch and hazel, but there are some planted conifers dotted about too. Slowly gain height and cross the first bridge.

As this dark but lush world begins to close in around you, you come to realise that **Stanley Ghyll** is quite unlike anything else in the Lake District. The steep sides of the gorge are dripping with mosses and ferns, some of which are rare; and, even when the outside world is cool, you can feel the humidity rising.

After the second railed bridge, climb a flight of steps over Stanley Ghyll. At the top, the main route heads right. However, if you want to get up-close and personal with **Stanley Ghyll Force**, continue beyond the third and final bridge. As the signs point out, however, the next short section of path is on slippery rocks with

Stanley Ghyll Force

a steep drop into the ravine. Confident walkers – with good soles on their boots – will be treated to an uninterrupted view of the 18m sliver of whitewater gushing down through a hidden gap in the almost black rocks.

After viewing the waterfall, retrace your steps to rejoin the main route by taking a path to the left, just before the second bridge. This then zig-zags its way out of the gorge. Don't cross the small clapper-like bridge; instead, turn sharp right again. The narrow path begins descending through the trees. Keep right at a fork close to a gate, dropping more steeply now. On reaching the beckside path, turn left and retrace your steps to the gate out of the woods. Turn right along the track, soon passing the junction of bridleways you passed earlier.

The track later becomes a lane that crosses Trough House Bridge over a lovely gorge on the River Esk. On reaching a T-junction with the main valley road, turn right. The station is about 300m ahead on the left.

WATERFALLS

Depending on the definition used, there are dozens, even hundreds of waterfalls scattered throughout the Lake District National Park. Several are visited on routes in this book, including Tom Gill (see Walk 1), Stockghyll Force (Walk 10), Sour Milk Ghyll (Walk 12), Stanley Ghyll Force (Walk 14) and Aira Force (Walk 27).

Many of the waterfalls in the Lake District are a dramatic by-product of the last glacial period – the result of the powerful interplay of ice and rock creating 'hanging valleys'. A good example can be found in Borrowdale: the Lodore Falls on Watendlath Beck (see Walks 21 and 22). Watendlath Beck's hanging valley was gouged out by a tributary to the main Borrowdale glacier, and so didn't erode as deeply. The difference in levels is exaggerated by the Skiddaw slates of the main valley being eroded more quickly than the Borrowdale volcanics, on which the beck lies. The result is that the upper section of the beck 'hangs' above the level of the glaciated valley floor (Borrowdale), dropping dramatically, via the waterfall, as it reaches the main valley.

Given perpetual life by the region's high rainfall, the waterfalls come thundering off the fells in a variety of forms: from gently cascading becks and elegant ribbon-like falls to deafening surges of churning whitewater. Many carry the name 'force'. Like the words fell, beck, dale and tarn, this is derived from an old Norse word, foss, in this case simply meaning 'waterfall'.

Walk 15

Upper Eskdale

The drama builds with every step you take on this sublime walk to the National Park's most remote dalehead. Here, a vast amphitheatre awaits, surrounded by high, craggy mountains, including Scafell Pike and Bow Fell. Only the hardiest of fell-walkers visit this lonely but exquisite spot. The waterproof quality of your boots will be put to the test as, high in the valley, the route ventures on to the edge of the Great Moss and then fords the River Esk.

Bow Fell over the head of Eskdale

Start/finish	Small parking area just E of the cattle grid at the bottom of Hardknott Pass, about 4km E of Boot (NY 213 011)
Distance	13.4km (8¼ miles)
Total ascent	425m (1400ft)
Grade	3/4
Walking time	4½hrs
Terrain	Mostly clear paths, but damp and indistinct in upper valley
Maps	OS Explorer OL6; or OS Landranger 89
Refreshments	Woolpack Inn, near Boot
Transport	None

Leaving the parking area, walk down the road and take the track on the right, leading to **Brotherilkeld Farm**. Just before the gate into the farmyard, bear left.

The monks of **Furness Abbey** in south Cumbria bought more than 5500 hectares of Upper Eskdale, including Brotherilkeld Farm, in 1242. They farmed sheep here, and possibly cattle. The lord of the manor, who had his hunting rights in mind, made sure that when the monks built their enclosure walls they kept them at a height that allowed deer to leap across.

At first, the path runs along a narrow stretch of land between fields and the **River Esk**, but the route then breaks out into more open country. Bow Fell magnificently fills the view ahead, acting like a rocky beacon, tempting walkers

The River Esk in its early stages

on into the upper reaches of the valley. After a ladder stile, there are no more walls between you and those alluring mountains.

The path is reasonably clear, maintaining some height above the river at first. Then, about 300m beyond the stile, it drops closer to the water's edge. As you head upstream, there are lots of delicious, aquamarine pools – popular with bathers on hot summer weekends. Local legend has it that the Everest mountaineer Tenzing Norgay lost his false teeth while swimming in the pools near Lingcove Bridge.

Cross the bridge over **Lingcove Beck** and continue upstream beside the River Esk on your left. With the

river thundering through a deep, dark gorge, this is a particularly dramatic section of the valley. The river itself, although only a few metres below, is rarely visible from the main path because the gully sides are so steep.

Crinkle Crags puts in an appearance to the right before Throstlehow Crag blocks the view, but it's the scene ahead that soon grabs the attention: as the gradient eases, Scafell Pike and Ill Crag appear – a grey, desolate jumble of bare rock and scree poking up above the grassy slopes straight ahead.

As you near a sharp river bend to the left, the path swings away from the Esk slightly. At the first chance, head north to the base of the crags of **Scar Lathing**. This will involve crossing a small stretch of boggy ground.

Turn left along the clear path at the base of Scar Lathing. The path and river soon swing north again and the mountains ringing Eskdale appear: Scafell Pike, Ill Crag, Esk Pike, Bow Fell and Crinkle Crags. Stretched out ahead, carpeting the flat expanse at the valley head, is the **Great Moss**, a vast area of bog.

Scafell Pike and Ill Crag appear – a grey, desolate jumble of bare rock and scree

On reaching the edge of the Great Moss, head north north-west along a faint, stony path, aiming for a grassy knoll that provides some dry going after the initially wet path. A fairly clear path continues beyond this knoll until you draw level with Sampson's Stones, the huge boulders on the other side of the river. Now, you need to negotiate a boggy area and cross a deep, but narrow beck. Beyond, a faint trail leads through the grass, making straight for the river. Walk upstream for about 200m – until you encounter the end of a tumbledown wall. Carefully ford the River Esk here.

Once on the west bank, head towards the foot of the pencil-thin waterfall of **Cam Spout**. Before you reach the falls, you'll see a faint, grassy path cutting across your route. Turn left along this. The path skirts the base of the boulder-strewn slopes, keeping to level ground until it climbs between Sampson's Stones, some of which serve as shelters.

After going through a gap in a wall near a sheepfold, the path becomes more obvious. It is rough but crosses mostly level ground, losing only a little height as it passes beneath **Silverybield Crag**. About 800m beyond this crag, the path skirts the edge of another boggy area by hugging a small lump of rock on the right. Watch carefully for an indistinct path that climbs on to the rock. This then heads west before resuming its route south, bypassing some very soggy ground in the process.

The path later descends into the valley on broad, sweeping curves. Don't be tempted by a faint path to the left as you near a wall close to the bottom of the slope; simply follow the wall down to Scale Bridge. There is a pretty waterfall just above the bridge.

About 80m beyond the bridge, as the wall swings down to the left, keep straight ahead to cross the higher of two ladder stiles. (This one is to the left of a wooden gate.) Continue straight ahead with the wall on your left until you reach a gate close to the farm buildings at **Taw House**. Go through the gate and turn right along the track.

Just after the gate to the tiny stone cottage of Bird How, go through a small gate on the left – signposted Whahouse Bridge. Bear diagonally right to a gap in the wall in the field bottom. Continue parallel with the fence on your left to reach the road. Turn left to return to the parking area in 1km.

Walk 16

Hardknott Fort and Harter Fell

Harter Fell may be only 649m high, but the way its craggy outline towers over Eskdale, you'd be forgiven for thinking this knobbly peak was much higher. This walk first pays a visit to the Lake District's most spectacularly located Roman remains: the substantial walls of Hardknott Fort sit high up on a grassy spur about 250m above Eskdale with views across to the Scafell range. Those views – and more besides – dominate much of the walk as you then climb to the summit of Harter Fell. The ascent is mostly on grass, but the steeper descent negotiates rougher ground.

Hardknott Fort sits on a grassy spur above Eskdale

Start/finish	Small parking area just E of the cattle grid at the bottom of Hardknott Pass, about 4km E of Boot (NY 213 011)
Distance	6.8km (4¼ miles)
Total ascent	565m (1854ft)
Grade	4/5
Walking time	4hrs
Terrain	Mostly open fell with indistinct paths, boggy at times; steep, rough descent
Maps	OS Explorer OL6; or OS Landrangers 89 and 96
Refreshments	Woolpack Inn, near Boot
Transport	None

From the parking area, turn right and walk up the road for about 300m – until you see a squat fingerpost on the left. Turn left here. The path keeps close to the wall at first as it ascends to the south-west gate of **Hardknott Fort**.

Built at the beginning of the second century AD by the Emperor Hadrian, **Hardknott Fort** (Mediobogdum) housed 500 infantry soldiers from Croatia, Bosnia-Herzegovina and Montenegro. Living at 250m above sea level, they guarded the Roman road between Ambleside and Ravenglass. The thick fort walls are still in place and some of the internal structures have been partly rebuilt from fallen masonry. These include the commandant's house, the headquarters, a pair of granaries and the external bath house.

Having explored the substantial remains, leave the fort through the north-east gate.

On the climb on to Harter Fell. From left, Esk Pike, Bow Fell and Crinkle Crags

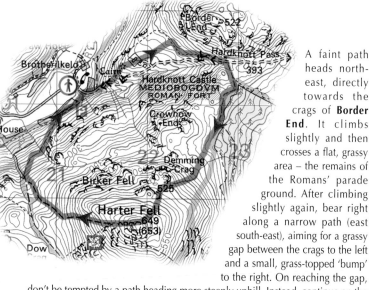

A faint path heads north-east, directly towards the crags of **Border End**. It climbs slightly and then crosses a flat, grassy area – the remains of the Romans' parade ground. After climbing slightly again, bear right along a narrow path (east south-east), aiming for a grassy gap between the crags to the left and a small, grass-topped 'bump' to the right. On reaching the gap, don't be tempted by a path heading more steeply uphill. Instead, continue on the faint trail that follows the line of a grassy ledge at the base of the fell. Eventually, this rejoins the road at a sharp bend.

Turn left and walk uphill on the asphalt until, just before the pass proper, you reach a public bridleway fingerpost. Turn right here. Just a few metres beyond the road, bear right at a fork. You'll soon see a fence on the right; the faint, grassy track meanders to a gate in this fence about 300m south of where you left the road. Almost immediately after going through this, the grassy track swings sharp left. You'll then see another fence on your left. Follow the line of this fence (south south-west), ignoring a small gate where the bridleway enters forestry land.

Crossing some soggy ground along the way, reach a stile at a fence corner. Cross this and turn right. The faint path follows the fence on your right at first, but then swings left. After leaving the security of the fence, it heads south south-east for about 100m and then swings south-west to begin its moderate ascent of the grassy fellside.

This is not a well-used path, so you may lose sight of it at times; if this happens, simply head south-west to reach the summit of Harter Fell. As you climb, take some time to turn around and savour the ever-improving views of the Scafell range and the other magnificent mountains at the head of Eskdale. Don't be fooled into thinking **Harter Fell** is the dome of rock you can see straight ahead as you briefly follow a small beck upstream. That's actually Demming Crag. Harter

Looking north-west from the summit of Harter Fell

Fell's summit consists of a collection of jagged crags and rocky outcrops. The trig pillar sits on some rocks in the north-west corner of the summit area, but the true summit lies just a few metres to the east.

The views from **Harter Fell** on a clear day are simply stunning. The Lake District's highest mountains dominate the scene to the north and, out to the west, the Isle of Man seems to be no more than a quick swim away. Looking down on to the Hardknott Pass road (north), you also get an impressive bird's eye view of the Roman fort.

Come back down from the rocks housing the trig pillar, take a few strides south, descend right and then quickly swing right along a clearer path (west). Your descent steepens as you pass a cairn. About 125m beyond the cairn, ignore a path heading left; keep to the cairned route (west north-west). Eventually, towards the base of the fell, you'll be joined by a path from the left. Continue downhill in a north-westerly direction. Having descended to an area of grass and bracken, you'll see a fence straight ahead. Do not go right up to it; instead, about 150m before reaching it, bear right at a grassy fork (north north-west).

You finally reach the fence near its junction with a wall. Turn right along the clear track and through a gate in the wall. Continue downhill on the wide bridleway with the pyramid-like peak of Bow Fell dominating the head of **Eskdale** ahead.

Having dropped into the main valley, go through two kissing-gates in quick succession. Descend a rough path to cross Hardknott Gill via Jubilee Bridge, which is just below the parking area where the walk started.

THE ROMANS IN THE LAKE DISTRICT

Cumbria was on the north-western edge of the mighty Roman Empire. The invaders arrived in Britain in AD43 and by AD71 had managed to subdue the Celtic tribes of northern England, but the Picts of mountainous Caledonia, or Scotland, were another matter entirely. So, it was in Cumbria in AD122 that Emperor Hadrian, realising the Picts would never be governed by Roman rule, decided to mark the Empire's border with a massive defensive structure – now known as Hadrian's Wall.

Because of its strategic position on the edge of empire, Cumbria was purely a military zone. The 20th-century historian Professor RG Collingwood once described the county as being 'almost at vanishing point in the scale of Romanisation'. As such, although there is plenty of evidence of Roman roads, forts and other defensive structures, you won't find villas or markets or even Roman place names. But the military establishment was an impressive one and many of the forts survive today, as do the roads that link them. Hardknott is one of the most dramatically located forts, high above Eskdale on the road linking the port of Ravenglass with another fort on the northern shores of Windermere at Ambleside. The Roman road crossed the Hardknott and Wrynose passes, and the modern road, with its many hairpin bends, still uses part of it. Other Roman remains in the Lake District include High Street, the road crossing the high fells between Brougham and Ambleside, and the bathhouse at Ravenglass.

Walk 17

Loweswater Corpse Road

For relatively little effort and using clear, generally well-signposted bridleways, this walk provides superb views of Loweswater and the surrounding fells. There is a gentle climb near the beginning, but after that, you're on a wide, easy-to-follow track high above the lake. The return route is via quiet lanes and a pleasant woodland path beside the lake. Don't forget to take a picnic – there's a bench almost halfway through the walk where you can sit and enjoy the wonderful scene.

Looking across Loweswater to Whiteside, left, and Grasmoor

Start/finish	Maggie's Bridge car park near Loweswater (NY 134 210)
Distance	8.8km (5½ miles)
Total ascent	270m (890ft)
Grade	1/2
Walking time	3¼hrs
Terrain	Indistinct paths at first; good track; farm paths; lanes; woodland trails
Maps	OS Explorer OL4; or OS Landranger 89
Refreshments	Kirkstile Inn, Loweswater
Transport	None

Take the rough track heading south-west from the car park's entrance – towards **High Nook Farm**. The fell straight ahead is Carling Knott and the old Corpse Road, which forms such an important part of this walk, hugs its north-east face. Walk through the yard, passing the farmhouse on your left and then out through another gate. Heading gently uphill with Highnook Beck down to your right, keep to the clear track next to the drystone wall on your left.

After a gate in a wall, keep to the clear, slightly stony track until it ends. Now veer right on a less obvious path over potentially muddy

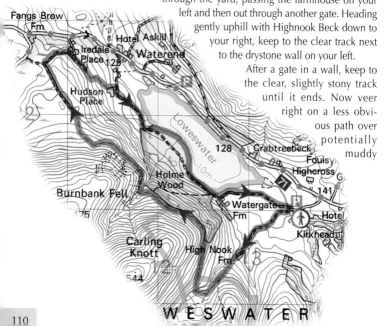

The High Nook track provides good views back to Darling Fell, left, and Low Fell

ground. After crossing **Highnook Beck**, the path swings right and climbs gently. You've now turned your back on the low-lying fells to the south of Loweswater; over to your right are the more dramatic mountains on the other side of the Lorton Vale, including Whiteside and Grasmoor.

After a few minutes of fairly gentle uphill work, the path levels off slightly and you reach the edge of a conifer plantation. A few minutes on the level is soon replaced by more uphill work, after which you go through a gate and the views open out again. You can see the Irish Sea far ahead, and, before long, you also catch glimpses of Loweswater through the trees. The lovely, grassy track drops to cross Holme Beck and then continues its undulating way around the side of **Burnbank Fell**.

Up until the 17th century, as Loweswater had no burial ground, **coffins** had to be carried on horseback along this bridleway to Lamplugh and then on to St Bees Abbey for burial. Despite its morbid beginnings as a corpse road, it's a delightful path and it now has the added benefit of a well-placed bench just to the right, which affords some wonderful views down Loweswater and Crummock Water.

CORPSE ROADS

In medieval times, when the population was more thinly scattered that it is today, people often had to travel long distances to get to their nearest church – and that applied in death as well as in life. When a corpse needed to be buried, it would be strapped on to a sled or pony's back and carried, often for many kilometres, to the nearest consecrated burial ground. For Loweswater, for example, the parish church was at St Bees, more than 20km away. For the inhabitants of Garrigill in east Cumbria, their final journey climbed to 780m as it passed close to the summit of Cross Fell, the highest point on the Pennines. The routes used by the funeral parties became known as 'corpse roads' and some of them were used as such until the 18th century. Indeed, many still exist today as bridleways, such as the one linking Grasmere and Ambleside (see Walk 11) and the Loweswater route.

Inevitably, Cumbria's corpse roads have various legends associated with them. Before St Olaf's Church at Wasdale Head was licensed for burials, coffins had to be carried on horseback to St Catherine's in Eskdale. On one stormy winter's day, the horse carrying the coffin of a young local man suddenly took fright and disappeared into the mist near lonely Burnmoor Tarn. It was never seen again. Another local story involves the rowan, a tree said to have restorative properties. As one coffin was being carried from Wasdale to Eskdale, it hit a rowan tree and the dead woman inside was revived.

Loweswater from the Corpse Road

Beyond a bench, the track climbs gently to a gate and ladder stile. It then heads downhill, passing through another three gates as it does so. When it swings sharp left, leave the track by turning right over a ladder stile or through the two gates – signposted Hudson Place. Keeping close to the wall on the right, the grassy path becomes more track-like as it descends. At a junction with a surfaced lane, turn right and then right again along a rough track near the cottages at Jenkinson Place.

Soon after the next gate, follow the faint but broad, grassy path half-left. In the next field, walk with a row of gnarled trees on your left. Cross a double stile at another gate and head towards **Hudson Place**. Just before the buildings, go through the gate on your left. Now keep close to the fence on the right to reach the next gate.

Once through this gate, turn right along the lane, soon passing in front of the buildings of Hudson Place. Two gates mark the end of the lane just after the farmhouse; go through the left-hand one, looking straight down on to shimmering Loweswater. At the bottom of this narrow path, cross the gate/stile to access a track through **Holme Wood**. Take the surfaced path on the left in a short while to enjoy a lovely lakeside stroll. This path later rejoins the main woodland track just beyond the stone-built bunkhouse.

The mixed woodland here is full of life compared with the dense conifers that you saw from the corpse road – birdlife is plentiful and you stand a good chance of seeing a **red squirrel**. Cumbria is one of the last strongholds of this native breed, which has been replaced in most of England and Wales by the grey squirrel, introduced from North America in 1876. There are estimated to be only 140,000 red squirrels left in the whole of Britain – most of which live in Scotland – compared with more than 2.5 million greys.

After leaving the woods via a gate, the track heads towards **Watergate Farm** and then swings left to return to the Maggie's Bridge car park.

Walk 18

Buttermere

For an easy walk in magnificent surroundings, look no further than the circuit of Buttermere. This little lake, probably one of the most photographed in the Lake District, is ringed by spectacular mountain scenery. And, with mostly good paths underfoot, you'll have plenty of time to enjoy the views.

Looking across Buttermere to Hassness and Goat Crag

Start/finish	Pay-and-display car park behind the Bridge Hotel in Buttermere (NY 173 169)
Distance	6.9km (4¼ miles)
Total ascent	95m (305ft)
Grade	1
Walking time	1¾hrs
Terrain	Lakeside paths and tracks; short section of road walking
Maps	OS Explorer OL4; or OS Landranger 89
Refreshments	Croft House Café, Bridge Hotel and Fish Inn in Buttermere
Transport	Bus 77/77A, summer only

Leaving the car park, bear right along the public bridleway to the left of the Fish Inn. Keep to this wide track as it winds its way to the lakeshore. After a gate providing access to the shore, turn right, soon crossing the outlet stream via a bridge. Cross a second bridge, go through the gate and then follow the lakeshore path. Keep left at any forks, so that you have uninterrupted views across the lake.

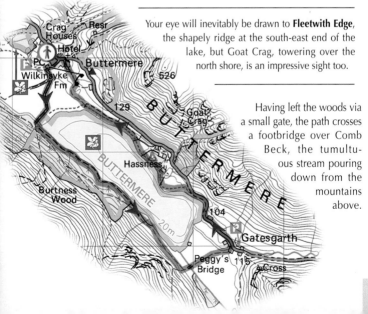

Your eye will inevitably be drawn to **Fleetwith Edge**, the shapely ridge at the south-east end of the lake, but Goat Crag, towering over the north shore, is an impressive sight too.

Having left the woods via a small gate, the path crosses a footbridge over Comb Beck, the tumultuous stream pouring down from the mountains above.

115

The south east end of Buttermere

Keep left as a trail heads uphill to the right in a short while. Before long, you reach a junction of paths at a gate. Go left through the gate and follow the wide track to **Gatesgarth Farm**. Turn left along the road, keeping into the side and being particularly careful on the bends. After about 600m of road walking, you regain the lakeshore. Take the gravel path to the left in a short while.

This makes its way along the lakeshore, back towards the village, below **Hassness** and passing through a short, dark tunnel that has been cut into the rock along the way. When you reach the western end of the lake, go through a small gate. Ignore the gate on the left here providing access to a shingle beach; simply keep straight ahead. The path goes through a series of gates and passes between the buildings of **Wilkinsyke Farm** to reach the road just below the tiny church in Buttermere. Turn left and then left again just before the Bridge Hotel. The entrance to the car park is now on the right.

MARY ROBINSON – THE BEAUTY OF BUTTERMERE

The Fish Inn was home, 200 years ago, to Mary Robinson, the 'Beauty of Buttermere' made famous in Melvyn Bragg's novel *The Maid of Buttermere*. She became a celebrity in 1792 when Captain J Budworth wrote about her in his *Fortnight's Ramble to the Lakes*, saying: 'Her hair was thick and long, of a dark brown and, though unadorned with ringlets, did not seem to want them; her face was a fine oval, with full eyes and lips as red as vermilion.' Consequently, she received many noteworthy visitors, including Wordsworth.

In 1802 an apparently prosperous tourist arrived in Keswick – Colonel the Honourable Alexander Augustus Hope, MP for Linlithgow and brother of Lord Hopetoun. He seduced Mary and married her at nearby Lorton. When the newspapers reported the wedding, Scottish readers pointed out that the real Colonel Hope was in Vienna. Mary had married an imposter – John Hatfield, a linen draper's traveller who was wanted for forgery and bigamy. He had married two women previously, abandoning them when their money started running low. He had also been signing documents in the guise of an MP. He was arrested in Cumbria but escaped, eventually reaching Wales where he was caught. Although Mary refused to testify against him, he was tried in Carlisle and hanged in 1803 for forgery. Mary later married a Caldbeck farmer.

Walk 19

Crummock Water and Rannerdale Knotts

Its setting may not be as dramatic as that of its more famous neighbour to the south-east, but, in so many other ways, the beauty of Crummock Water far surpasses Buttermere's. Yet you'll find fewer walkers attempting a circuit of this serene, atmospheric lake. There are two reasons for this: firstly, Crummock Water is larger than Buttermere and, secondly, there are some damp paths to negotiate along its western shore. As long as neither of these factors puts you off, you're in for one of the best lakeside experiences the Lake District has to offer. But first, this walk heads on to the gorgeous, grassy ridge of little Rannerdale Knotts (355m) for a spectacular view of the lake.

Grasmoor from the shores of Crummock Water

Start/finish	Pay-and-display car park behind the Bridge Hotel in Buttermere (NY 173 169)
Distance	14.3km (9 miles)
Total ascent	570m (1870ft)
Grade	3/4
Walking time	4¾hrs
Terrain	Woodland paths; low, grassy fell; valley trail; lakeshore path, wet in places; tracks
Maps	OS Explorer OL4; or OS Landranger 89
Refreshments	Croft House Café, Bridge Hotel and Fish Inn in Buttermere
Transport	Bus 77/77A, summer only

From the car park, head back out on to the road, turn left and then, almost immediately, go through the small gate on your right. A path leads through a narrow stand of attractive oak woodland beside Mill Beck. Faced with a choice of path, always go for the higher option.

Leave the woods via a flight of wooden steps and a gate. Cross diagonally left to pick up a narrow trail heading uphill through the bracken, bearing right at a fork after just a few strides. At a crossing of paths, turn right along a broad, grassy

Crummock Water from Rannerdale Knotts

swathe. As the gradient eases, take the narrow trail on the left, climbing at a gentler angle now. With your first glimpse of Crummock Water ahead, you soon join the main path along the grassy ridge of **Rannerdale Knotts**. Bear left here. Follow this lovely ridge as far as you wish, but eventually you'll have to retrace your steps. The highest point at the western end is marked by a small cairn.

When you finally turn round and head back, watch for the point at which you first came up on to the ridge. A few metres after passing it, bear left on to a narrower path and then left again at the bottom of the drop in **Rannerdale**.

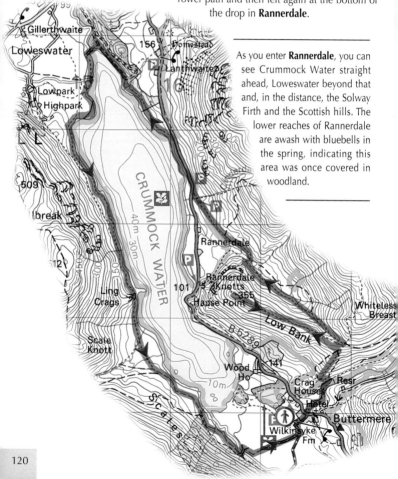

As you enter **Rannerdale**, you can see Crummock Water straight ahead, Loweswater beyond that and, in the distance, the Solway Firth and the Scottish hills. The lower reaches of Rannerdale are awash with bluebells in the spring, indicating this area was once covered in woodland.

Looking across Crummock Water to Melbreak

Approaching the west end of the tiny valley, the path goes through a gate. Cross the footbridge here and bear left to join a broad path continuing downstream. About 1km beyond the bridge, ford a beck above a small parking area. Drop to the road here, turn right and walk along the asphalt for about 200m – until you see a kissing-gate in the wall to your left. Go through this.

Heading downhill with a wall on your left, pick up a clear path that swings right – along the shore of **Crummock Water**. You later enter private woodland via a small, metal gate. Beyond the next stile, carefully ford a beck and then go through a kissing-gate to enter **Lanthwaite Wood**, a pleasanter area of mixed woodland belonging to the National Trust.

Nearing the west end of the lake, bear left to drop to a couple of benches close to the water's edge. As the path swings south-west, cross two footbridges in quick succession and continue along the gorgeous lakeside path. After a third bridge, the views become even more impressive as you look straight down the lake towards Red Pike and the High Stile range. The path goes through a gate to the right of an old pumphouse.

After the next kissing-gate, the onward path isn't obvious at first, but keep close to the shore and, before too long, all will become clear again. After crossing a beach and going through a gate, head south-east along the lake's shore. The route is wet in places, particularly in the early stages, but stones have been laid on top of the soggiest sections.

Above you now are the steep, unwelcoming slopes of Mellbreak, a brooding fell standing aloof from its neighbours. On the other side of the water is the mighty Grasmoor, its western face dissected by crags and gullies that hide some of the most famous scrambles in the Lake District.

Jutting out into the lake about two-thirds of the way along this shore is the grassy promontory of **Low Ling Crag**. At the end of the 18th century, when carriages could get no further than Hause Point at the base of Rannerdale Knotts, tourists would take a boat from near the coaching inn at Scale Hill to this narrow spit of land. From here, they would walk to Scale Force and then on to Buttermere before returning, by boat, to the carriages that awaited them at Hause Point.

Keep to the shore path and, eventually, as the slopes to your right ease back a little, you reach a bridge. Cross this and go through the gate on the other side. A clear path heads through the bracken to cross a second bridge. In their attempts to negotiate the boggy ground ahead, walkers have created a mess of parallel paths. Whichever you choose, make sure you don't gain too much height. The general direction is south-east as you keep about 200m back from the lakeshore. Before long, you join a constructed path and your difficulties are over.

The path crosses another two wooden footbridges before you finally say good-bye to Crummock Water and the slopes to your right begin to close in again. Take the next turning on the left, crossing the gated humpback bridge over **Buttermere Dubs**. Follow the clear track to its junction with an even wider one, along which you turn left. This soon swings right – leading back into Buttermere. The car park is on the left immediately after the Fish Inn.

NORTHERN LAKE DISTRICT
*Keswick, Borrowdale
and Derwentwater*

On the delightful valley path below High Rigg (Walk 23)

Walk 20

Walla Crag and Great Wood

This lovely walks starts with an easy wander across open fell to Walla Crag and one of the very best views of Derwentwater. It is followed by a gorgeous stroll through ancient woods and along the base of the fells to return to the car park near the ever popular Ashness Bridge.

Looking out over Derwentwater from the path to Walla Crag

Start/finish	Small cark park a few metres S of Ashness Bridge (NY 269 196)
Distance	7.1km (4½ miles)
Total ascent	385m (1266ft)
Grade	2
Walking time	2½hrs
Terrain	Clear path on open fell; quiet lane; woodland tracks/trails
Maps	OS Explorer OL4; or OS Landranger 89 or 90
Refreshments	Choice of cafés, pubs and restaurants in nearby Keswick
Transport	The nearby Borrowdale road is served by the 78 bus and, in summer, the 77/77A

Turn left out of the car park and then, almost immediately, turn right along a signposted footpath with a wall on your right. About 130m beyond the first stile, turn left to cross Barrow Beck via a footbridge. A reasonably clear footpath now climbs to a gate, beyond which you are on a lovely, gently

Ashness Bridge

rising track above **Derwentwater**. On a clear, sunny day, the views across the lake to the Derwent Fells are pretty special.

At the top of Cat Gill, close to the summit of Walla Crag, is a steep gully called **Lady's Rake**. This is reputedly the route by which Lady Derwentwater fled from her home on Derwentwater's Lord's Island on hearing of the impending execution of her husband, James Radcliffe. Radcliffe was the third and last Earl of Derwentwater, a member of one of the prominent local families who had adhered to the Catholic faith and supported the Jacobites in the 1715 rebellion.

The Highlanders, proclaiming James Stuart as king, got as far as Preston where they were forced to surrender. Radcliffe admitted his involvement with the uprising when he appeared before the Privy Council in January 1716, and begged for mercy, blaming his participation in the uprising on youth and inexperience. But his mitigation couldn't save him and he was executed on Tower Hill.

Reaching a stile in a wall, cross it for the final pull on to **Walla Crag**.

This is another fantastic **vantage point**. Looking from the left, you can see up into Borrowdale, Derwentwater below, Bassenthwaite Lake – far beyond that is Criffel in Dumfries & Galloway – then Skiddaw and Blencathra.

Having taken in the view, head away from the top in a north-easterly direction to follow a path that skirts the edge of the crag and drops to a gate. Go through and turn left along a wide, grassy path. With a wall on your left, you plunge downhill and through a gate to gain access to a clear track.

Drop to a narrow bridge. Crossing **Brockle Beck** here, turn left along the surfaced lane for 200m and then left again down a footpath – signposted Keswick and Great Wood. Recross Brockle Beck via a narrow footbridge and then turn right, heading downstream.

About 300m beyond this bridge – and just above a radio mast – turn left along a clear path.

This soon leads into **Great Wood** and joins a wider track from the right. Continue in the same direction and, after almost 1.4km, turn left at a T-junction. When the path splits – just after reaching a paved section – bear right to cross Cat

The bracken-bronzed slopes on the other side of Derwentwater belong to Cat Bells

Gill via a narrow bridge. The clear path now heads downhill with a wall on the right for a while before swinging left across more open ground at the foot of the cliffs of **Falcon Crag**.

At a fork in the path, bear left. After going through a gate in a drystone wall, drop on to the road. Turn left and you'll soon cross Ashness Bridge. The car park is now just a few metres ahead on the right.

Walk 21
Derwentwater circuit

The circuit of Derwentwater can be anything you want it to be: you can turn it into a café crawl by stopping at the many coffee shops and hotels passed as you make your way around this gorgeous lake or, if you're feeling tired, you can always cut the walk short and get the boat back to Keswick at any one of several piers. The best time of year to see the lake is autumn when the woods and fells surrounding it are at their colourful best. The trees are various shades of red, golden and auburn, while the bracken, as it slowly dies back, creates a beautiful, bronzed backdrop to the scene.

Derwentwater and Skiddaw

Start/finish	Pay-and-display car park next to the Theatre by the Lake in Keswick (NY 265 229)
Distance	14.2km (8¾ miles)
Total ascent	330m (1076ft)
Grade	1/2
Walking time	4¼hrs
Terrain	Mostly good lakeside paths and tracks; risk of flooding
Maps	OS Explorer OL4; or OS Landranger 89 or 90
Refreshments	Choice of cafés, pubs and restaurants in Keswick and at various points around the lake
Transport	Keswick is well served by buses. There are regular services between the town and Cockermouth, Workington, Penrith, Carlisle, Grasmere, Ambleside, Windermere, Kendal and Lancaster.
Note	If the lake level is high, some paths on the E side of Derwentwater flood. After particularly wet weather, you may have to walk into Grange to get round the S end of the lake. This will add 3.2km to the distance.

Turn left out of the car park and walk down the lane, soon with Derwentwater and the ferry's landing stages on your right. Keep straight ahead whenever the path forks and walk to the end of **Friar's Crag** for some great views down the lake.

Cat Bells and Maiden Moor seen from the shores of Derwentwater

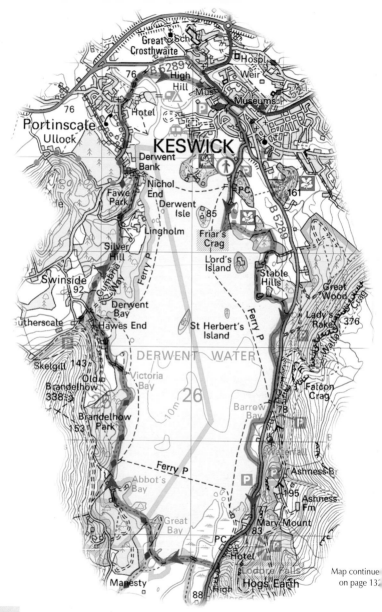

Great
Crosthwaite

Great Sch

Hospl

Weir

B 5289

76

High
Hill

Mus

Museums

Hotel

76

P

P

P

Portinscale

Ullock

KESWICK

Derwent
Bank

161

PC

B 5289

Nichol
End

Fawe
Park

Derwent
Isle

85

Derwent
Isle

Lingholm

Friar's
Crag

Silver
Hill

Lord's
Island

Stable
Hills

Great
Wood

Swinside

92

Cumbria Way

Derwent
Bay

St Herbert's
Island

Ferry P

Lady's
Rake

376

Gutherscate

Hawes End

Skelgill 143

DERWENT   WATER

Victoria
Bay

Old
Brandelhow
338

26

Falcon
Crag

Barrow
Bay

78

Brandelhow
153
Park

10m

P

Ferry P

Abbot's
Bay

Ashness Br

P

P

195

Ashness
Fm

Great
Bay

Mary Mount

83

PC

Map continue
on page 132

Hotel

Lodore Falls

Manesty

88

High

Hogs Earth

Friar's Crag is believed to be so-called because it was the embarkation point for monks making a pilgrimage to St Herbert's Island. Today, it is more closely associated with **John Ruskin**. He first visited the Lake District when he was five. He once said that the 'first thing I remember as an event in life was being taken by my nurse to the brow of Friar's Crag on Derwentwater'. It was, he continued, 'the creation of the world for me'.

One of the most influential thinkers of his age, Ruskin wrote more than 250 works on subjects as diverse as literary criticism, social theory, the history of art, mythology, ornithology and pollution. His ideas, which contained a strong desire to improve conditions for the poor, had a profound effect on the early development of the Labour Party in Britain. There is a memorial to him among the trees on the crag.

Turn round to retrace your steps, and then, almost immediately, take a narrow trail on the right heading up to Ruskin's Monument. Keep right, descending a few steps, and then turn right through a gate. The path now winds its way along the lakeshore. Just after a bench on the far side of this open area, there are two gates leading into

A stroll through Derwentwater's woods

the trees. Use either of these. At a T-junction, turn right, later returning to the lakeshore.

As the path brushes up against the wall beside the road, you could cross the wall to walk beside the road – this avoids a craggy section in a short while. Alternatively, continue on the lake side of the wall. Eventually though, some small crags will prevent you from continuing along the water's edge. You now have no choice but to climb to the road. Carefully clamber up the crag and turn right along the roadside path.

On reaching the turning to Watendlath and Ashness Bridge on the left, go through the gap in the wall on the right to access the lakeshore again. (If the water level is too high, continue along the road to the Kettlewell car park.) Turn left along the stony beach, soon passing through a gate. On reaching the Kettlewell car park, cross the road and go through the gap in the wall opposite to pick up a path through the woods.

Keep right whenever the path splits, and, after about 500 metres, you'll come back out on to the road. Turn left along the asphalt, past the Lodore Falls Hotel.

About 200m beyond the hotel, go through the large gate on your right – signposted Manesty. A good track leads to the footbridge over the **River Derwent**.

Detour if the south end of Derwentwater is flooded

If this track is flooded, you may be able to reach the bridge via a signposted path on the right just after the Borrowdale Hotel, which is a little further along the road. If this too is flooded, continue along the road to Grange, turning right over the road bridge. Walk through the village and then go through a wooden gate – signposted Lodore – on your right about 550m after passing the Borrowdale Gates Hotel. Having passed through another two gates, you

THE GERMAN MINERS

Walk anywhere in the Lake District, but particularly in the Derwentwater and Borrowdale areas, and you'll inevitably come across the remains of the mining industry. It may be in the form of spoil heaps, fenced shafts, open adits (horizontal mine openings) or abandoned buildings; or it may simply be the tracks, once used by miners and quarrymen, that are now trodden by walkers.

The scars left by mineral exploitation have almost all been created since 1564. This was the year that Elizabeth I invited German miners to England to help her find the metals she so desperately needed. One of the most important of these metals, initially at least, was copper. With the Spanish knocking at the door, she needed it to make cannons as well as for the minting of coins. Nobody in Europe at the time could locate the ore, extract it and then smelt the copper like the Germans could, so they were encouraged to come to England.

Employed by the Company of Mines Royal, they soon established both copper and lead mines throughout Cumbria, the centre of their operations being Keswick. At first, there was some discord between the immigrants and the locals – some of the Germans even decided to establish their own, relatively safe settlement on what is now known as Derwent Isle – but the miners brought prosperity and a touch of the exotic to the area. By 1600, at least 60 miners had married local women. Their anglicised family names, including Stanger and Hindmarch, are still common in the area today.

reach more open ground; bear left here and then right after some boardwalk. Turn left along a gravel path, rejoining the main route 500m beyond the footbridge over the River Derwent.

The route around the south end of the lake is a combination of gravel path and boardwalk. Beyond a gate in a drystone wall you enter woodland. On reaching a narrow lane at The Warren, turn right. Bear left at a fork and then, just after passing beneath a cottage, bear right to drop to a gate. The path hugs the lakeshore and then re-enters the woods near High Brandelhow Pier. As it does so, keep to the path closest to the water.

The woodland here is known as **Brandelhow Park**, and it was the National Trust's first Lake District acquisition. It was bought by public subscription in 1902 to prevent housing development. Princess Louise, Queen Victoria's daughter, presided over the official opening. After the ceremony, Princess Louise and the three National Trust founders – Hardwicke Rawnsley, Robert Hunter and Octavia Hill – each planted an oak tree.

At the next pier – Low Brandelhow – go through the gate. Facing a choice of two wide, surfaced tracks, take the one on the left. Turn right along a surfaced lane and then right again in front of **Hawes End** outdoor centre.

A few metres after passing the path down to Hawes End Jetty, go through a small gate on the right. After crossing an open area, go straight over a rough track. At a lane near the entrance to **Lingholm**, cross diagonally left to continue on the path towards Keswick – beside a wall and then a fence on the right. Having crossed one more surfaced lane, drop to **Nichol End Marine**. Turn left here and then right at the road.

Walk into **Portinscale** and take the first road on the right. At the end of the lane, cross the suspension bridge and, after 100m, turn right to access a fenced path. Turn left on reaching a lane and then turn right at the main road. Go right at the mini-roundabout in **Keswick** and follow the road round to the left. At Howe Keld Hotel, turn right along The Heads. Keep left when the road splits and then turn right at the café to return to the car park.

Walk 22

A Borrowdale ramble

This route gives walkers a chance to meander through beautiful Borrowdale, enjoying the valley from a variety of angles. It follows riverside trails, weaves its way in and out of woodland, climbs to the summit of Castle Crag (290m), flirts with the shores of Derwentwater, pays a visit to the Lodore Falls and climbs to lonely Watendlath, where the temptation to take a coffee-and-cake break will be hard to resist. Set off on a crisp, sunny morning and then take your time, savouring all that this fine dale has to offer.

Castle Crag

Start/finish	National Trust pay-and-display car park in Rosthwaite (NY 257 148)
Distance	16km (10 miles)
Total ascent	645m (2122ft)
Grade	4
Walking time	5hrs
Terrain	Tracks; woodland trails; steep in places; risk of flooding
Maps	OS Explorer OL4; or OS Landranger 89 or 90
Refreshments	Several hotels, cafés and pubs along the route, including at Seatoller, Watendlath and Rosthwaite
Transport	78 bus and, in summer, the 77/77A
Note	If the lake level is high, you may have to walk into Grange to get round the south end of the lake, but this will not add to the total distance.

From the car park in Rosthwaite, turn right along the lane, soon passing the Flock-In tearoom. Follow the track to the **River Derwent** and cross via New Bridge. Turn left along the riverside path, joining a surfaced lane close to the next bridge over the river. Keep to the west side of the river, briefly swinging away from the water to pass directly in front of the hostel buildings. Beyond this, continue straight ahead on a riverside path through the woods. A couple of short sections of bare rock have to be negotiated after the next gate. Don't be tempted to head up to the right just yet; keep to the water's edge until a fence forces you to turn away.

Keep to the clear path as it meanders its way in and out of the woods. It eventually passes through a large gate and drops into the car park at **Seatoller**. From the car park

The tiny settlement of Watendlath

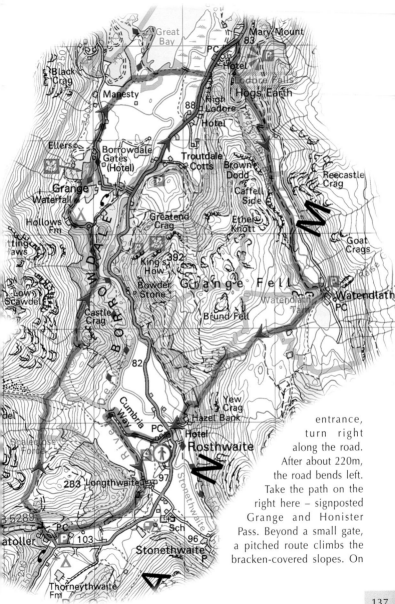

Mary Mount
83
PC
Great Bay
Hotel
Lodore Falls
Black Crag
Hogs Earth
Manesty
High Lodore
88
Hotel
Ellers
Borrowdale Gates (Hotel)
Troutdale Cotts
Brown Dodd
Reecastle Crag
Grange
Caffell Side
Waterfall
Greatend Crag
Ethel Knott
Hollows Fm
Goat Crags
tting aws
King's How
392
Grange Fell
Low Scawdel
Bowder Stone
Watendath
Watendlath
PC
Castle Crag
Brund Fell
82
Cumbria Way
Yew Crag
Hazel Bank
PC
Hotel
entrance, turn right along the road. After about 220m, the road bends left. Take the path on the right here – signposted Grange and Honister Pass. Beyond a small gate, a pitched route climbs the bracken-covered slopes. On
Rosthwaite
283 Longthwaite
97
Stonethwaite
PC
atoller
P 103
Sch
96
P
Stonethwaite
Thorneythwaite Fm

A glorious view of Borrowdale from Castle Crag

reaching a track, cross diagonally left to continue uphill on a broad, grassy path leading to a gate in a wall. Go through this and turn right.

Hugging the base of the fells, this excellent path provides spectacular views towards Skiddaw, Castle Crag and Grange Fell. From this side, Castle Crag appears to be dominated by a half-dome of bare, grey rock, but as you get closer you can see that it is, in fact, a huge pile of slate. A little later, you'll be climbing up through this. For the time being, simply stride out and enjoy the scenery.

Almost 1.5km after first joining this path, you meet a wider track from the left. In a further 120m – just before the track starts descending – take a faint path to the right. This passes beneath a small, dark crag and climbs to a low grassy ridge. Walk with the fence on your right to reach a wall. Cross the stile on the right and then the ladder stile. Turn right along a path just ahead.

You soon reach the base of the steep, slate path that zig-zags its way uphill at **Castle Crag**. At the top of the first part of the climb, you come to the old quarry workings that created this mess on the hillside. The deep green of the valley bottom will inevitably draw your eye south-east. A less obvious path climbs to the right of the workings to reach the summit of this little hill. From here, Skiddaw and Derwentwater dominate the scene, a fitting place for the memorial on the summit crag.

Sir William Hamer gave **Castle Crag** to the National Trust in 1920 in memory of his son and 10 other men from Borrowdale who were killed during World War One. The fell is crowned by the remains of an Iron Age hill fort. The Romans also used it, probably taking advantage of its prominent, strategic position within the valley.

But Castle Crag has been occupied more recently than that. Between the two world wars, two of its caves became the summer home of Millican Dalton. Sick of being a commuter in southern England, he migrated north to the Lake District on an annual basis, making ends meet by leading walking parties on the fells and making tents and rucksacks. He turned one cave into a living area and one into a bedroom, which he called 'The Attic'.

Retrace your steps back towards the ladder stile at the base of Castle Crag, but instead of climbing it, follow the path round to the right. Go through a small gate, and follow the path down to a clear track. Turn right, enjoying the views of Skiddaw while you can because, after the next gate, you enter woodland.

Bear right at a fork to cross a bridge over a tiny beck. As you near the River Derwent, head left to recross the beck via a lower bridge. Follow the Derwent downstream, soon crossing yet another small bridge.

On reaching a rough track, turn right and then go left at a surfaced lane – signposted Manesty. The route passes through the yard of **Hollows Farm**. The track continues and then narrows before reaching a wooden gate among the trees. Once through this, swing right along a stony path. At a path junction next to a wall, turn right. Go through the gate to pick up a narrow trail that soon swings left, passing above **Grange**. It descends to the road opposite the **Borrowdale Gates Hotel**. Turn left here.

After walking along the asphalt for about 550m, turn right through a gate on to a clear path – signposted Lodore. After a kissing-gate, you reach a larger gate providing access to heathland close to the south end of Derwentwater. Bear right after this gate and then go right again along the clear, lakeshore path. A long section of boardwalk leads to a footbridge over the River Derwent after which the path continues to the main Borrowdale road.

Detour if the south end of Derwentwater is flooded

There is a chance, particularly in winter, of the south end of Derwentwater being flooded. In this case, as you come down to the road opposite the Borrowdale

Gates Hotel, you should turn right and then go left at the T-junction with the main Borrowdale road to pick up the walk description at the Lodore Falls Hotel.

Turn left and walk beside the road for 500m. Having passed the Lodore Falls Hotel, you'll see signposted routes leading into the woods on your right. Ignoring the path towards Keswick running almost parallel with the road, keep right. The path swings right, joining a route from the left. Nearing the Lodore Falls Hotel, ignore any lesser trails to the right – keep to the clearest route straight ahead. Before long, you'll reach a bench with a superb outlook over Watendlath Beck and the Lodore Falls. Head up to the left to reach a distinct fork at the base of the wooded slope. Bear left here.

Don't be tempted to head up to the right until the path you're on makes a decisive bend to the right. Then, where the gradient briefly eases, ignore the path straight ahead; instead, swing sharp left with the main trail. It performs one more bend to the right before reaching a stile. Beyond this, the trail continues uphill through the woods – more gently now.

At a junction with a clearer path – from where you can see Watendlath Beck sparkling through the trees – turn left. In a further 150m, take the narrow, stony

Watendlath Beck

trail on the left – easy to miss in the vegetation. This quickly climbs to a wider path, along which you turn left. Then turn right along a broad, stony path.

After a gate in a wall, turn right along a cobbled path. Turn left immediately after the bridge over **Watendlath Beck**. You are now on a pleasant beckside path which, after 2.1km, leads to Watendlath.

After the gate close to the small, stone bridge leading into the pretty little hamlet, the main route goes right, keeping **Watendlath Tarn** on your left. Only cross the bridge if you wish to make the short detour into Watendlath itself.

Watendlath was the setting for Hugh Walpole's 1931 novel *Judith Paris*. It was the second of four novels belonging to Walpole's **Herries Chronicle**. Set in Keswick, Borrowdale, Watendlath, Uldale and Ireby, these books tell the story of the Herries family from the 18th century to the depression of the 1930s.

When the track splits after the next gate, bear right – signposted Rosthwaite. The stony way crosses Puddingstone Bank and then descends. The impressive peaks on the skyline ahead include Great Gable, Great End and Scafell Pike. Losing height, you pass a kissing-gate on the right. Ignore this. Soon after, you go through a gate to continue downhill. Turn right to go through the next gate in a wall – signposted Rosthwaite.

Reaching the valley bottom, turn right to cross the bridge over Stonethwaite Beck. Go left at the road and then turn right to re-enter Rosthwaite. The car park is on the right just after the toilet block.

Walk 23

Castlerigg Stone Circle and High Rigg

High Rigg is a lovely little lump of fell – sometimes grassy, sometimes craggy – towered over by all its neighbours. Its highest point is just 357m above sea level, and yet it has much to offer: hidden tarns, dark crags, springs and becks galore, knobbly summits, even a short section of narrow, heather-covered ridge – it's like the Lake District in miniature. It makes a great introduction to fell-walking. This walk approaches High Rigg from the enigmatic Castlerigg Stone Circle, later dropping into the lightly wooded valley of St John's in the Vale and then returning via the open pastures of Low Rigg.

High Rigg from Castlerigg Stone Circle – with the Dodds and the Helvellyn range behind

Start/finish	Roadside parking beside Castlerigg Stone Circle, about 1.6km E of Keswick (NY 291 237)
Distance	13.5km (8½ miles)
Total ascent	560m (1845ft)
Grade	3/4
Walking time	4½hrs
Terrain	Farm paths; low fell; valley path; quiet lanes; short section beside busy main road; potentially very wet in places
Maps	OS Explorers OL4 and OL5; or OS Landranger 90
Refreshments	Low Bridge End Farm's garden and conservatory is open for drinks and light snacks
Transport	Bus 73A

From the parking area, face the field containing Castlerigg Stone Circle and turn left along the road. After 200m, go through the gate on the right – signposted High Nest. Walk parallel with the fence – then wall – on your right and go through a small gate on the other side of this field.

Continuing in roughly the same direction, go through another small gate at a kink in the wall opposite. Now aim to the right of the conifers ahead and, after one more gate, walk with the fence on your left.

Views of Blencathra figure highly on this walk

On the far side of this field, a rough track leads to **High Nest**. Follow the lane between the buildings and then go through a large gate to the left of a cattle grid – signposted A591 and St John's in Vale. The fence on the left guides you on and drops to a farm lane, along which you turn right.

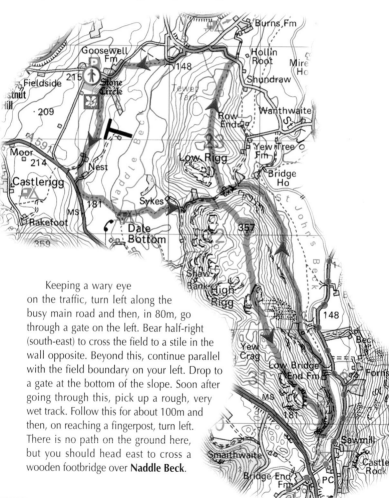

Keeping a wary eye on the traffic, turn left along the busy main road and then, in 80m, go through a gate on the left. Bear half-right (south-east) to cross the field to a stile in the wall opposite. Beyond this, continue parallel with the field boundary on your left. Drop to a gate at the bottom of the slope. Soon after going through this, pick up a rough, very wet track. Follow this for about 100m and then, on reaching a fingerpost, turn left. There is no path on the ground here, but you should head east to cross a wooden footbridge over **Naddle Beck**.

Go through the gap between the wall and the fence opposite, walk beside the fence on your left for 100m and then swing right to cross the field (east), exiting via a small gate. Follow the rocky outcrop uphill to a kissing-gate.

Turn right along the lane and then left to climb a rough, stony track. Just before a gate on the track, you will see a bench to the right. Turn right here – on a faint, grassy path climbing to the right of a small beck. You're now on the lower slopes of **High Rigg**. Cross the beck via a plank bridge and continue uphill for about 80m. At a brief lull in the climb, turn left. Bear right at a fork in a short while and then, at a crossing of paths, turn left. As the path steadily gains height, the view to the left is dominated by Skiddaw and Blencathra, divided by the Glenderaterra Beck.

When the crags of Clough Head appear ahead, excellently framed by a small dip in the ridge, you reach a T-junction. Turn right. In just a few seconds, the full grandeur of the setting is revealed as Thirlmere and the Helvellyn range appear to the south. High Rigg's summit cairn is up on the rocks to your right.

A path continues around the south side of the summit rocks and then drops left. Ignore a path to the right as you near a wall. The clear route continues beside this wall, briefly swinging away from it to bypass a tiny tarn.

Soon after crossing a ladder stile, bear left at a fork. Another secret tarn is discovered beyond a notch in the hill. Descending beside a fence, you soon have an excellent view of Thirlmere. Cross a stile in the fence and follow a clear path on to Long Band, a delightful section of heathery ridge. At the south end of it, the path drops left, descending loose ground. After passing through a gap in a wall, the route climbs again before descending through an area of Scots pines.

Eventually, you'll drop to a junction of trails near the base of the fell. Turn left here. A clear but narrow path passes high above **St John's Beck** before descending to valley level. What now follows is 3.2km of gentle valley walking, in and out of pretty woodland, often with excellent views of Blencathra ahead. Part-way along the valley, pass **Low Bridge End Farm**, where the lure of tea and cakes may prove irresistible.

Keeping close to the fence/wall on the right all the while, you'll eventually reach a road. Turn left and then, just after St John's Church, cross the stile on the right. Head away from the wall on a faint path and then turn right along a clearer path across **Low Rigg**. This soon swings left (north north-west), joining another path from the right.

After a wall stile, continue in the same direction. Reaching the top of a short rise, you'll see **Tewet Tarn** ahead. Aim to the right of this, crossing a stile in a fence on the way. A wall stile is crossed about 30m back from the water's edge. A faint path now heads north. On reaching a squat fingerpost, bear right (north-east) towards a wall corner. Follow the track downhill. After the gap in the wall, cross muddy ground to reach the wall on the right and then drop to a gate in the bottom right-hand corner of the field.

Turn left along the road and then left again at a T-junction – signposted Keswick. Take the next road on the left – signposted Castlerigg Stone Circle. Just after crossing Naddle Bridge, go through the gate on the left. Making your way up towards the white buildings of **Goosewell Farm**, go through the gate in the wall opposite. Bear left to enter a third field via another gate. Swing half-right, aiming directly for the farm. Entering the fourth and final field, continue in the same direction to a gate in the top wall. Turn left along the road and the parking area where the walk began is about 400m ahead on the right.

If you haven't already visited the stone circle, go through one of the small gates opposite the parking area to enter the field in which it is located.

Castlerigg is one of the oldest stone circles in the country, dating back to about 3000BC, the late Neolithic period. Nobody knows what the people of the New Stone Age would have used it for, although various theories have been put forward over the years. Was it an astronomical observatory? A religious site? Or maybe just a trading centre for hand axes? An interpretation panel near one of the gates explains the circle's history and shows a model of the stones as they are today.

Castlerigg Stone Circle

Outerside and Barrow

Coledale, to the west of Keswick, is surrounded on three sides by an impressive group of fells that includes Crag Hill, Hopegill Head and Grisedale Pike. But this spectacular valley isn't just about high, craggy mountains: sitting to the south of the main beck are three smaller hills that provide superb walking – Outerside (568m), Stile End (447m) and Barrow (455m). This walk climbs this excellent trio by first following Coledale Beck from Braithwaite to impressive Force Crag and then using an old, but little-used path beside Birkthwaite Beck to gain the higher ground. It's a great combination of dramatic valley walking and some surprisingly good low-level ridges.

Derwentwater, Walla Crag and, in the distance, the Dodds – all seen from Barrow

Start/finish	Royal Oak pub in Braithwaite, near Keswick (NY 231 236). Parking can be found, outside of school hours, in the nearby school car park; alternatively, there is roadside parking in the village
Distance	9.3km (5¾ miles)
Total ascent	580m (1910ft)
Grade	4
Walking time	3½hrs
Terrain	Valley track; less clear paths on open fell; ridge walking; quiet lane
Maps	OS Explorer OL4; or OS Landranger 90
Refreshments	Royal Oak, Middle Ruddings, Coledale Inn, Hobcartons tea room and Scotgate Holiday Park's tea room, all in Braithwaite
Transport	Buses X5 and, summer only, 77/77A

With your back to the pub, turn left along the main road. After 350m, just as the road swings right, take the path on the left – signposted Coledale Hause. On reaching a wide track, turn left.

Continuing upstream, you now have about 3km of easy track

Force Crag Mine, Coledale

walking ahead, an opportunity to enjoy the spectacular scenery of **Coledale**. To your left are the three small peaks that you will be climbing later: the furthest east is Barrow, then Stile End and finally Outerside.

Nearing the **Force Crag** mine workings, take the less well-maintained track dropping left to ford **Coledale Beck**.

A detour of 350m along the main track leads to mine workings, occupying an atmospheric spot with the ominous, almost vertical cliffs of Force Crag bearing down on them. **Force Crag Mine** was worked intermittently from Elizabethan times right up until the end of the 20th century. A lead vein was located at Coledale Head in 1578, although mining didn't start in earnest until the early part of the 19th century. The mill building that exists today was built in 1908.

The last attempt to extract ore was made by the New Coledale Mining Company in 1984, but the firm left in 1991. The mine was declared a Scheduled Ancient Monument in 2001 and the area is also a Site of Special Scientific Interest because of the variety of minerals found here. The National Trust bought the mine and its mineral rights in 1979 and now runs occasional tours of the site.

Beyond the beck, continue uphill on the clear track for about 430m. As the gradient eases slightly, watch for a small cairn. Turn left here – along a wide, grassy

From Barrow, looking back to Outerside and to the higher Coledale Fells beyond

path. This zig-zags its way up the fellside. After crossing **Birkthwaite Beck**, a narrower path continues to wiggle its way uphill – more steeply now. About 300m up from Birkthwaite Beck, a tiny cairn marks a faint fork. Bear left here. At the top of the short rise, you will see Outerside immediately ahead. After crossing some damp ground, bear left as another path joins from the right and climb on to **Outerside**.

The view to the left is dominated by shapely **Grisedale Pike**, but with a little more height, it's Skiddaw that grabs all the attention. From the summit, Bassenthwaite Lake, Blencathra, the Helvellyn range, Derwentwater and, in the distance, the North Pennines can also be seen.

From the top, continue down the other side of the fell on an obvious path. The heather-filled gap between Outerside and Stile End is a gorgeous carpet of purple when the heather blooms in late summer. As you cross a couple of damp,

peaty dips, keep straight ahead. At the second of these, you will be joined by a clearer path joining from the right. Soon after this, the path swings left – to skirt the edge of a boggy area – and then right, joining a path from the left. Nearing the top of the ensuing climb, bear left at a fork to reach the unmarked summit of **Stile End**.

Turn right and, with Barrow over to your left, drop to the shallow gap between the two fells, known as Barrow Door. Here you will encounter a clearer path; cross straight over this to begin the ascent of the pleasantly rocky south-west ridge of **Barrow**.

Descending the other side, keep to the apex until you drop off the far north-east end of the fell. Here, looking down on Braithwaite, turn left at a T-junction with a broad, grassy path. Go through a small gate and then through a wooden farm gate. Walk between the farm outbuildings – signposted Braithwaite – and then follow the farm track to the road.

Turn left along the road to walk back to the village. The Royal Oak, where the walk started, is on your right as you reach a T-junction.

Walk 25

Wythop's Fells

Ling Fell (373m) and Sale Fell (359m) are the two diminutive tops to the north of the Whinlatter forests. Using a combination of quiet lanes and some pleasant, easy-going hill tracks, this walk completes a partial circuit of both fells and pays a quick visit to their respective summits for some excellent views.

The empty expanse of Wythop Moss and Embleton High Common

Start/finish	Roadside parking 200m NE of St Margaret's Church, near Wythop Mill (NY 191 302)
Distance	11.8km (7¼ miles)
Total ascent	530m (1732ft)
Grade	3
Walking time	3½hrs
Terrain	Quiet lanes; hill tracks; open, grassy fell
Maps	OS Explorer OL4; or OS Landranger 89
Refreshments	The Pheasant Inn, Wythop
Transport	Bus X5 stops at Dubwath, about 1.6km from the start of the walk

From the parking area, walk south-west along the road, passing **St Margaret's Church** on the left. Walk straight through the charming old hamlet of **Wythop Mill**. The road now climbs. You will see a road on your left, signposted to the 'Old School'. About 200m after this, turn left along a rising track skirting the north-west base of Ling Fell – signposted Highside.

When the track begins to drop, you will see farm buildings below. Just before reaching them, go through the gate on your left – signposted Embleton High Common. A faint path climbs steadily beside

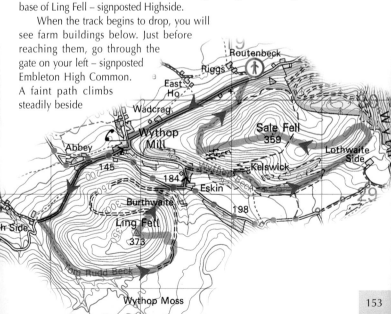

a fence on the right. Bear right on reaching a track. Having turned your back on the wooded valleys, you are now looking into the lonely heart of the forsaken hills and mires north of Whinlatter. The walk is already taking on an air of remoteness.

About 400m after losing the fence on your right, bear left at an obvious fork to continue on your circuit of the base of the fell. Dazzling quartzite boulders dot the south-west slopes of Ling Fell, one of them standing close to the path. The track peters out on its approach to a fence at Bladder Keld Spring. Go through the gate here. A path to the left just after the gate will lure you uphill, but you must resist; keep to the base of the fell, crossing damp ground at first and then walking with a fence on your immediate right. Close to a gate, join a grassy track that swings away from the fence. Sale Fell soon puts in an appearance directly ahead.

Teaming up with the fence again, you'll encounter a damp ditch. Just after this, the track becomes clearer and more solid. Step off the track here and head up through the bracken on your left to reach a wide grassy path about 50m above. Bear right (north) along this and then, in a further 100m, turn left along a clear path climbing the steep east slopes of **Ling Fell**.

From the trig pillar on **Ling Fell**, you are greeted by a fine outlook north-west: a scene that includes the Solway Firth, the Robin Rigg offshore windfarm and the hills of Dumfries & Galloway.

Trig pillar on Ling Fell

A rough track heads into Chapel Wood from Kelswick Farm

Several paths radiate out from the summit. The widest of these heads north. Take the narrower path to the right of this (north-east), which snakes its way downhill. Bear right when it splits, briefly heading east before veering north-east again. Go straight over a couple of path crossings and, descending more steeply now, eventually reach a clear track close to a wooded area. Turn left here and, at a junction of tracks close to a fence corner, turn right to descend to a gate. Go through this and turn right along the surfaced lane.

Take the next road on the left, and then turn right after Brumston Bridge. This asphalt lane climbs gently along the south-west base of Sale Fell and ends at **Kelswick Farm**. Just before the farm gate, turn right along a rough track – signposted Beck Wythop. You soon pass the site of Wythop's old church in a quiet, shady setting on the edge of Chapel Wood.

The old **Wythop church** was built in the middle of the 16th century and was demolished in 1865 when St Margaret's was built on the other side of Sale Fell. At one time, late in the building's life, the church bell was suspended from the branch of a tree. In August each year, an open-air service is still held near the ruins.

Looking across Bassenthwaite Lake to Skiddaw

The bridleway enters the atmospheric oak woods via a deer gate. Keep left along the level path at a faint fork. As the path climbs away from the woods, Skiddaw and its associated ridges loom large over the sheep-filled enclosures. At a faint fork, keep left along the higher, clearer path. With Bassenthwaite Lake clearly visible down to the right, the path passes through an area of gorse. Immediately after this – and about 100m back from a gate entering the forest – turn left to climb a steep, grassy slope.

Just after a tiny copse of gnarled old trees, bear left at a fork and then swing left on to a grassy ridge. This provides great views back across Bassenthwaite Lake towards Skiddaw. The springy, close-cropped turf makes for easy walking. Joined by a path coming up from the left, the broad, grassy path swings right (north-west) to pass through a small notch in the hillside. Ignoring a path to the left, keep straight on. Swing right on crossing the remains of an old wall and make your way up to a gated gap in a more substantial wall.

Go through the gap and keep straight ahead, climbing more steeply now. Before long, you reach the top of **Sale Fell**: the highest point marked by a flat area almost devoid of vegetation. Two broad, grassy paths head west: one just below an exposed rock face, the other above. Take either of these. Immediately after they reunite, they split again and you are able to take your pick again. They finally come back together just above a wall. Bear right along the track next to this wall.

About 500m after parting company with the wall on the left, the stony route appears to go over to grass. Bear left here, dropping through a gap in a wall and descending to the road opposite the roadside parking where the walk started.

EASTERN LAKE DISTRICT
Ullswater and Patterdale

Looking into Grisedale on a lovely late spring morning (Walk 26)

Walk 26

Grisedale and Lanty's Tarn

This walk visits Grisedale, the steep-sided, glacial valley that divides the Helvellyn range from Fairfield and its neighbours. As you progress upstream from Patterdale, the scenery gradually changes and the valley's walls close in around you. The return route pays a visit to Lanty's Tarn, a delightful pool surrounded by trees.

Place Fell seen from the start of the walk

Start/finish	George Starkey Hut, Patterdale (NY 394 160). There is room for a few cars to park in front of the building. Alternatively, the pay-and-display car park is 200m to the SE
Distance	11.6km (7¼ miles)
Total ascent	380m (1250ft)
Grade	2
Walking time	3½hrs
Terrain	Good valley paths and tracks; easy climb to tarn
Maps	OS Explorer OL5; or OS Landranger 90
Refreshments	White Lion Inn and the Patterdale Hotel, both in Patterdale; several bars and cafés in Glenridding
Transport	Buses 108 and, summer only, 508

With your back to the George Starkey Hut, turn left along the main road and then, after about 220m, turn right along the driveway of the **Patterdale Hotel**. Pass to the right of the building and then between the hotel and a smaller wooden outbuilding. Take the narrow path heading through the trees – beside a tiny beck. This is joined by a path coming up from the left and then goes through a gate to cross bracken-covered slopes.

A short climb provides a glimpse of Ullswater to the right, and there are superb views of Place Fell behind. After going through a kissing-gate, the clear path continues beside a wall. Cross Hag Beck via stepping stones. At the bottom of the path heading left on to Birks, you will see a small gate down to the right.

Ignore this, keeping straight ahead on a less clear path beside the fence and then a wall.

Another steady climb brings you to a gate in a wall. In another 60m, go

The glacial valley of Grisedale

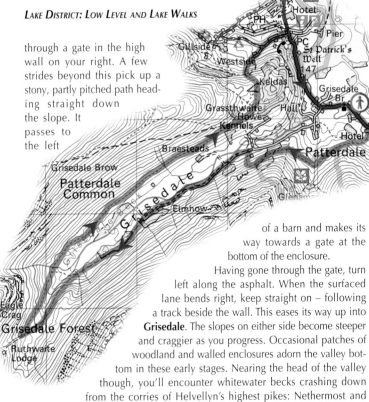

through a gate in the high wall on your right. A few strides beyond this pick up a stony, partly pitched path heading straight down the slope. It passes to the left

of a barn and makes its way towards a gate at the bottom of the enclosure.

Having gone through the gate, turn left along the asphalt. When the surfaced lane bends right, keep straight on – following a track beside the wall. This eases its way up into **Grisedale**. The slopes on either side become steeper and craggier as you progress. Occasional patches of woodland and walled enclosures adorn the valley bottom in these early stages. Nearing the head of the valley though, you'll encounter whitewater becks crashing down from the corries of Helvellyn's highest pikes: Nethermost and Dollywaggon.

As you draw level with Nethermostcove Beck on the other side of the valley, keep left as a faint path heads right to a wooden footbridge over Grisedale Beck. As the path continues along the south side of the beck, the valley becomes wilder and the climb steeper. The beck here flows through a narrow ravine, the waterfalls of which can be seen more clearly from the return path.

Ruthwaite Lodge, squatting on a grassy shelf beneath the formidable buttresses of Dollywaggon Pike ahead, used to be a shooting hut. Maintained by Outward Bound Ullswater, it is dedicated to two of the organisation's instructors who were killed on New Zealand's highest mountain, Mount Cook, in 1988.

Having crossed the next bridge over **Grisedale Beck**, the path swings right beside a subsidiary beck. Walkers could continue another 300m uphill to visit Ruthwaite Lodge, but the return route begins by crossing the bridge over this smaller beck about 250m after the Grisedale Beck crossing. The return path is a little rougher than the outward route, but it's still fairly straightforward. After passing beneath the lower crags of Helvellyn's pikes, it crosses a bridge over Nethermostcove Beck and then traverses gentler, bracken-covered slopes at the base of the mountains. Enormous boulders line the route, probably dumped here by the glacier that gouged this valley from the bedrock millennia ago. Some still bear the scars of the ice's abrasive forces.

Having passed above the farm at **Braesteads**, join a wider path from the left. Ignore the gate on the right here; simply keep straight ahead. Before long, you reach a fingerpost and the stony path begins climbing – signposted Lanty's Tarn. Keep to this broad path as it makes its way up to this small body of water.

Lanty's Tarn was named after Lancelot Dobson, whose family owned much of Grisedale in the 18th century. The tarn was later enlarged by the Marshall family, who lived at Patterdale Hall. They fished here and also built themselves an ice house where they stored ice for use in the summer.

Lanty's Tarn

The path descends towards Glenridding

Go through the gate at the far end of the tarn and follow the clear path through the bracken. The path descends to a gate. Don't go through this; instead, swing right with the clear path. After a kissing-gate, descend through the trees. Nearing the bottom of the slope, bear right at a waymarker post. Go through a gate, over a small bridge and along a fenced section of path to come out near a cottage. Turn right along the track, soon joining a path from the left – signposted Glenridding Bridge.

Turn right on reaching the main road through **Glenridding**. There are roadside paths all the way back to the George Starkey Hut in Patterdale – sometimes to the right of the asphalt, sometimes to the left. Be careful when crossing.

Walk 27

Aira Force and Gowbarrow

After a walk through the magnificent Aira Gorge, home to another of the Lake District's impressive waterfalls, this route heads on to Gowbarrow Fell (481m). The scene from the top is great, but it's only after following a path around the eastern side of the fell that this diminutive hill reveals its true glory: a breathtaking view of Ullswater that, in my opinion, cannot be beaten.

The western expanse of Ullswater is suddenly revealed as the path rounds the south side of Gowbarrow

Start/finish	National Trust car park beside Aira Force near the junction of the A5091 and A592 (NY 400 200)
Distance	6.7km (4 miles)
Total ascent	400m (1315ft)
Grade	2/3
Walking time	2½hrs
Terrain	Clear path through woodland; open fell; muddy in places
Maps	OS Explorer OL5; or OS Landranger 90
Refreshments	Tearoom in car park
Transport	Bus 108

Take the path at the far end of the car park and keep right at a fork. After a gate, turn left, away from the iron railings. Ignoring a trail on the left, you'll soon climb with **Aira Beck** on your right. About 500m into the walk, descend a steep stone staircase on your right to the base of **Aira Force**, feeling the spray from the powerful waterfall even on calm days. Cross the bridge and turn left – up another set of stone steps.

At the top, as you meet a path from the right, a tiny detour to the left will take you to a humpback bridge across the top of the waterfall: a noisy, dramatic spot after heavy rain. Back on the main path, continue upstream with the beck close by on your left, later joining another path from the right and then passing **High Force**.

The trees begin to thin out and then disappear entirely after a small gate. Just before reaching the next, larger gate, turn right on to a faint path that ascends to

a gate. Beyond this, the climb up the western slopes of **Gowbarrow Fell** begins. It's steep at times, but there is stone pitching to ease your progress in places.

Trig pillar on Gowbarrow

Looking back, from the way up Gowbarrow

Having followed the line of the wall on your left for about 700m, the path, surfaced now, trends right – towards the trig pillar. Reaching a junction of paths at the base of the heathery summit knoll, turn right. The path quickly swings left to reach the trig pillar.

The hills lining the distant horizon to the east are the **North Pennines**, the highest tops along England's backbone; stacking up to the south-east are the many layered ridges of the Eastern Fells. It's a great view, but there's even better to come…

Looking south from the summit

Pick up a muddy trail heading north-east from the trig pillar to drop on to a surfaced path, along which you turn right. This winds its way through the bracken and heather on the north-east side of Gowbarrow, eventually reaching the scant remains of an old shooting hut. A wonderful section of the route now swings right, soon traversing steep slopes on a good path high above sparkling Ullswater.

About 1.2km beyond the ruins of the shooting hut, you round a bend in the path and are suddenly greeted by one of the most magnificent panoramas in the Eastern Lakes. The western expanse of Ullswater is revealed, blue and inviting, with the dark, craggy Helvellyn range forming the perfect backdrop. Another 45m and you come to a perfectly placed bench, a chance to sit and admire. It's an inspiring scene.

Far below, at the base of Gowbarrow, is another inspiring scene: the woodland here is said to have stirred **William Wordsworth** to write his most famous poem. Having walked through the woods with him on 15 April 1802, his sister Dorothy noted in her diary: 'I never saw daffodils so beautiful they grew among the mossy stones about and about them, some rested their heads upon these stones as on a pillow for weariness and the rest tossed and reeled and danced and seemed as if they verily laughed with the wind that blew upon them over the lake, they looked so gay ever dancing, ever changing.' Two years later, he used Dorothy's observations as the basis of a poem, the first line of which is probably one of the most famous lines in English poetry: 'I wandered lonely as a cloud.'

With the amazing view of Ullswater directly ahead, the path soon begins to descend. The apparently medieval tower below is known as Lyulph's Tower, but it's not as old as it first looks; it was actually built as a shooting lodge in 1780.

You eventually reach a junction of paths close to the edge of the fenced woodland at Aira Gorge. Go through the small gate to the left and then keep left as you descend, past a magnificent sitka spruce. After crossing a bridge over Aira Beck, you find yourself in an area of ancient yews with a couple of monkey puzzle trees (Chilean pines) towering over these native conifers.

The huge sitka spruce, planted in 1846, now has a girth of six metres. Many of the trees in this **arboretum** were planted by the Howard family of Greystoke. They were lords of the manor here from the late Middle Ages until they sold the land to the National Trust in 1906.

Keep left at any path junctions to return to the car park where the walk started.

Walk 28

Steel Knotts and Hallin Fell

*Steel Knotts is a lonely, low-level ridge close to the north-east edge of the
National Park. Thanks to its obscurity and its distance from the honeypots,
there's a good chance you'll have it all to yourself. From Howtown,
there's an energetic, but short pull to the 432m summit with its excellent
views of Martindale. And if it's views you crave, you'll not want to miss
out on the second summit of the day: little Hallin Fell. It may be only
388m above sea level, but an amazing panorama of lake and mountains
is dramatically revealed as you reach its summit obelisk. In between the
two, the route drops back to valley level. The return, around the base of
Hallin Fell, makes use of the lovely lakeshore path beside Ullswater.*

On the lakeside path around the side of Hallin Fell

Start/finish	St Peter's Church in Martindale, 7km SW of Pooley Bridge (NY 435 191)
Distance	9.5km (6 miles)
Total ascent	590m (1940ft)
Grade	4
Walking time	3hrs
Terrain	Open fell, pathless at times; quiet lanes; lakeside path
Maps	OS Explorer OL5; or OS Landranger 90
Refreshments	Howtown Hotel in Howtown; otherwise, nearest pubs and cafés are in Pooley Bridge
Transport	None

Climb the steep, grassy bank behind St Peter's Church. At the top of the rise, bear right at the faint fork. Dropping down the other side, bear left when the path forks again. Before long, you join a clearer track from the right. Follow this lovely

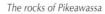

The rocks of Pikeawassa

Looking to the valley head from Pikeawassa

bridleway along the base of Steel Knotts with views of Howtown and Ullswater ahead.

After about 450m on this track, a wall comes up from the left. As this meets the bridleway, turn right along a very faint, sometimes muddy trail climbing the north-east ridge of **Steel Knotts**. The path is just to the right of a small rocky outcrop, but it can be hard to make out, especially in summer when it is hidden by bracken. Although the ascent is only short, it's steep in places. Beyond the cairn marking the first summit, stride out along the gorgeous ridge path towards the tor-like rocky outcrop marking the true summit, known as **Pikeawassa**.

From Pikeawassa, the head of **Bannerdale** looks a lonely, forlorn place while the rough slopes of Rampsgill Head seem harsh and uninviting. To your left are the steep, eastern slopes of Fusedale, rising towards Loadpot Hill, while the scene to the right includes Beda Fell and Place Fell. You may not have climbed much, but the scenery is truly magnificent.

Beyond the top, continue in roughly the same direction to drop down the grassy slope to a wall. Cross this via a well-camouflaged stile, and then walk with the wall on your left for about 130m. Ignoring a trail to the left, keep to the path as it veers away from the wall to meet a more obvious track. Turn sharp right here, almost back on yourself. The route quickly passes through a gap in a wall. It later descends steeply to drop into the valley to the right of **St Martin's Church**.

There are two **churches** in Martindale – the 'new' church of St Peter's, where the walk starts and finishes, and the tiny, isolated church of St Martin's. The latter, built in 1634, is lit by candle because it doesn't have electricity. St Peter's was built in 1882 to replace the older church. A storm is said to have destroyed the roof of St Martin's on the very day that St Peter's was consecrated.

Turn right along the road. Take the next road on the left. The walk can be cut short here by ignoring this turning and following the road back to St Peter's Church, 320m ahead. At the next road junction, close to the bridge over Howegrain Beck, go straight across to pick up a track to **Hallin Bank**. About 70m along this, take the path rising steeply to the right. Go straight over another path close to a gate in the wall/fence.

Before long, you find yourself on a wide strip of bracken-covered ground between two walls. As you near the top end of these walls, the path forks. To miss out the climb on to Hallin Fell, bear left to join a clearer path keeping close to the wall on the left. To stick with the main route, keep right at the first fork and then, ignoring any subsequent paths to the right, make your way straight up the fell (north). Gaining height, the narrow path fades and eventually disappears. Keep heading north and you'll eventually see two small, rocky knolls ahead. Aim for the gap between these. Here, join the well-worn, conventional route on to **Hallin Fell**. Follow this up and round to the right to reach the obelisk at the summit.

Obelisk on Hallin Fell

From the **summit** Ullswater stretches away towards lower-lying, gentler country to the north-east while, to the south-west, the mountains of the Helvellyn range provide a more rugged outlook.

Having rested, retrace your steps back towards the broad gap between the two walls. You're unlikely to be able to find the trail you took on to the fell, so follow the main path for about 180m and then, soon after it swings left, use your compass to strike south, descending steeply. On reaching a clear path just above the wall gap, turn right. You are soon walking with a wall on your immediate left. It is here that those who missed out Hallin Fell rejoin the main route.

Keep close to the wall, later entering Hallinhag Wood via a kissing-gate. The route descends to the lakeside path, along which you turn right. After emerging from the trees and later swinging away from the lakeshore, pass a small gate in the wall on your left. Bear right at a fork soon after this. On reaching the road, turn right. St Peter's Church, where the walk started, is about 200m ahead.

Walk 29

Ullswater shore

Ullswater is the second largest lake in the National Park, curling from the Eastern Fells to within a stone's throw of Penrith. This linear walk, making use of the Ullswater 'Steamer', follows its glorious shore along the base of the fells from Howtown to Glenridding. At first, gentle green slopes run down to the lake, but as you make your way south, the views become craggier and more dramatic. For an impressive finale, the route comes away from the well-trodden route and visits juniper-clad Silver Crag.

Silver Bay

Start	Howtown 'steamer' pier (NY 443 199)
Finish	Glenridding 'steamer' pier (NY 390 169)
Distance	11.3km (7 miles)
Total ascent	380m (1246ft)
Grade	2
Walking time	3hrs
Terrain	Lakeside paths and tracks; roadside path
Maps	OS Explorer OL5; or OS Landranger 90
Refreshments	Howtown Hotel in Howtown; several bars and cafés in Glenridding
Transport	Ullswater 'Steamers' (www.ullswater-steamers.co.uk)

Get off the boat at **Howtown** and turn right at the end of the pier to cross the footbridge – signposted Sandwick. After a short section of lakeside path, you go through two small gates to reach a rough lane, along which you turn right. Follow this for about 60m and then go through the gate on the left – still signposted Sandwick. The path soon climbs to a gate in a wall. Once through this, turn right to join the path around the base of **Hallin Fell**. Before long, you'll see the dark waters of Ullswater below.

After the next gate, keep to the lakeshore path through Hallinhag Wood. Ignoring any trails heading up into the trees on the left, you eventually leave the

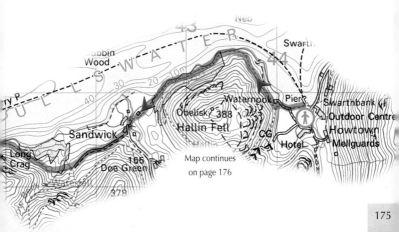

Map continues
on page 176

The Ullswater shore path

woods via a kissing-gate. The path soon climbs away from the lakeshore, crossing several meadows. It then bends sharp left as it approaches Sandwick Beck. Having crossed the bridge over the beck, turn left up the lane through the peaceful hamlet of **Sandwick**.

Take the path on the right immediately after Townhead Cottage. This soon joins another from the left and continues beside a drystone wall along the base of **Sleet Fell**. The path eventually draws closer to the water's edge again. The path gains a small rise among the light birch woods, after which the rocks to the right of the path provide a

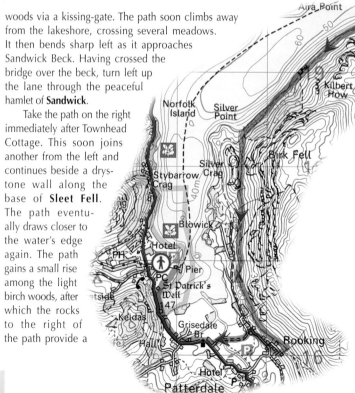

JUNIPER

The Lake District used to be covered in huge forests of juniper, but only small, isolated stands survive today, including the one on Silver Crag.

A decline in the use and management of juniper in recent years, coupled with reduced seed production of older plants and overgrazing of young saplings, has taken its toll on the increasingly rare evergreen – one of the UK's three native conifers. Sadly, it is also now under threat from a fungus-like organism called *Phytophthora austrocedrae*, first discovered in the UK in 2011. This pathogen infects the plant through the root system and causes the foliage to decline and eventually die.

In a recent survey, 231 juniper sites were identified throughout Cumbria. Wildlife groups are attempting to improve these sites and create new stands by planting thousands of saplings. In Longsleddale a few years ago, rock-climbers were brought in to plant juniper on inaccessible crags where they would be safe from sheep.

In the 17th century, the herbalist Nicholas Culpepper recommended juniper berries as a treatment for asthma and sciatica. He also claimed they could speed up childbirth. For several centuries, juniper berries have been used to flavour gin. Squash one of the berries between your fingers and then sniff – there's no mistaking that smell.

More crucially, on an ecological scale, juniper berries provide an important source of food for birds and animals such as field mice, squirrels and badgers.

Looking across Ullswater towards Glenridding from Silver Crag

superb view of Silver Bay and Silver Point directly ahead with the mighty mountains of the Helvellyn range behind.

Emerging from the trees near Silver Bay, you'll see a small, shingle beach down to the right. Now watch carefully for a pitched path rising steeply on the left. This climbs at a moderate angle to a secret valley between **Silver Crag** on your right and **Birk Fell** on your left. In summer, this spot is something of a sylvan gap in the mountains, but, in winter, bitingly cold winds cut through here, making it feel quite wild.

For a short detour on to **Silver Crag**, take a faint trail on the right as you approach the south end of this gap. When this splits, bear right again to climb quickly to the summit. A narrow path fights it way through the forest of juniper covering the top, but it's worth the effort for the views. Retrace your steps back to the gap and turn right.

A gorgeous grassy path now stretches out in front of you. Follow it as it traverses the fellside. You'll eventually pass an old green bench, beyond which the path drops slightly, passing some dramatic old quarry workings on the way. Approaching slate piles at the next set of workings, the path forks. Take either branch, although the one to the left is slightly easier.

Before long, the path forks again above some cottages. Turn right here, crossing a tiny bridge. Go through the large gate to gain access to the top of a lane. Turn right along the rough farm track. On reaching **Side Farm**, turn left between the buildings – signposted Glenridding.

Turn right on reaching the main road. There are roadside paths all the way back to Glenridding – sometimes to the right of the asphalt, sometimes to the left. As you cross back to the eastern side of the road close to the boat hire shed at St Patrick's Landing, go through the small gate to pick up a lakeside path. This comes out on to the lane leading to the Glenridding 'steamer' pier car park. Turn right to enter the car park.

Walk 30

Ullswater and The Cockpit

After a tranquil lakeside stroll from Pooley Bridge, this walk heads for the hills, climbing gradually on to low fells above the northern end of Ullswater. As well as being 'big sky' country, with some wonderful views across to the North Pennines, this atmospheric moorland is covered in mysterious Bronze Age remains, including The Cockpit stone circle.

View of Ullswater

Start/finish	Granny Dowbekin's Tearooms, Pooley Bridge (NY 470 244)
Distance	9.2km (5¾ miles)
Total ascent	215m (710ft)
Grade	2
Walking time	2¾hrs
Terrain	Lakeside trail; farm paths; boggy section; grassy moorland
Maps	OS Explorer OL5; or OS Landranger 90
Refreshments	Choice of cafés and pubs in Pooley Bridge
Transport	Bus 108

Standing with your back to Granny Dowbekin's Tearooms in Pooley Bridge, look straight across the road and you will see two driveways: one leading into the main car park, the other a private driveway to **Eusemere Lodge**. Cross the road and take the latter. Bear right at a fork – signposted Waterside House.

After going through a gate, the track follows the **River Eamont** to the edge of Ullswater and then along the wooded shore. Before too long, you leave the trees behind and are treated to wonderful, uninterrupted views down the lake towards Hallin Fell, Place Fell and the Helvellyn range.

Sometimes, the path is a constructed, gravel affair; occasionally, it deteriorates and becomes less obvious as its crosses areas of grass and pebbly beach; at one point, near Gale Bay, it crosses a long stretch of boardwalk.

The lakeside path finally ends when you reach the white farmhouse at **Waterside House Campsite**. Turn left here and then right along the road. On reaching the entrance to Ullswater Yacht Club on your right, turn left along the access track for **Seat Farm**. (This is the second track turning on the left after you join the road.) Turn right at the farm – signposted Howtown Road via Crook-a-dyke.

Immediately after going through a large wooden gate, go through a smaller gate over to the left. Follow the fenced path around the edge of the field. The path then crosses a wall stile next to a gate and continues with the wall on your right. It then swings left, fords a beck and goes through a small gate.

Make your way towards the farm buildings and pick up a clear track. Follow this for about 100m and then go through the kissing-gate on the left – signposted Howtown and Martindale. There are several faint trails just beyond the gate. Take the one heading south south-east – making directly for the steep slopes of **Barton Fell**. This winds its way between clumps of gorse as it negotiates the damp, often muddy ground of Sharrow Mire. Any time you are faced with a fork, bear right. The faint path swings south and then south-west as it begins climbing dryer ground, making for a small area of woodland just beneath **Auterstone Crag**. Walk

On the track below Barton Fell

The stone circle is hard to make out on the grassy moor

with the woodland wall on your right for a while and then, on reaching a clearer path, turn left up the open fellside.

As the path gently ascends, take some time to rest and enjoy the **views behind**: the dark waters of Ullswater with the even darker slopes of the Helvellyn range as a sublime backdrop. You'll have seen them before on this walk, but you can never get enough of a good thing.

Just after passing a fenced underground reservoir, ignore a grassy path up to the right. Keep to the clear path until you reach a fingerpost at the far end of a 500m stretch of wall. Swing right here to drop into the gill and cross **Aik Beck**. A clear track continues on the other side, crossing the open moorland. Keep right at a faint fork – staying on a mostly level path. You will soon see the Pennines in the distance. Look out too for **The Cockpit stone circle**, which you should be able to spot straight ahead, hiding in the grass. The path, stonier now, bends sharp left as it passes to the left of the stone circle.

The Cockpit stone circle

The Cockpit is one of several enigmatic features on this moorland thought to have been constructed during the Bronze Age. It is about 30m in diameter with standing or recumbent stones raised on the inside of a low bank. The tallest is almost 1m high. Other prehistoric features nearby include several smaller stone circles, a standing stone, burial cairns and at least one stone row.

Turn left at the next clear junction, heading downhill on a broad track. It's a lovely, gradual descent, providing yet another irresistible view down Ullswater. When the track ends, go through the gate and follow the lane to the edge of Pooley Bridge. Go straight over at the crossroads and then left at the mini-roundabout. The tearoom where the walk started is about 300m ahead on the right.

THE BRONZE AGE

There are Bronze Age remains scattered throughout the Lake District, including two that are visited on walks in this book: Swinside and The Cockpit stone circles. Many date from the early to mid-Bronze Age – roughly 2500BC to 1200BC – when the climate was considerably warmer, dryer and less windy that it is today, allowing people to move higher on to the fells. It is not unusual to find cairnfields and even settlements at almost 300m above sea level. Barnscar near Devoke Water and Burnmoor above Eskdale are among the 60 or so sites that have been excavated at this height.

Bronze Age people lived in round houses, grouped together in small settlements. They were farmers, keeping livestock and developing Britain's first field systems, growing mostly wheat and barley. And, of course, they were the first people to use metallurgy to create tools and ornaments. Today, these settlements are often on lonely, boggy moorland – places that see few visitors. They were abandoned in the late Bronze Age (around 1000BC) when the climate became cooler and wetter.

Bronze Age remains in Cumbria include hut circles, stone rows, standing stones, burial cairns and stone circles. Many of the cairns have been excavated and found to contain cremations, animal bones and antlers. But it is the stone circles that create the most intrigue. Why did Bronze Age people build these enduring monuments and what did they use them for? Were they religious sites, trading posts, calendars? We may never know for sure.

APPENDIX A

Useful contacts

Tourist Information Centres

Bowness-on-Windermere
Glebe Road
Bowness-on-Windermere
LA23 3HJ
Tel: 0845 901 0845

Keswick
Moot Hall
Keswick
CA12 5JR
Tel: 0845 901 0845

Ullswater
Beckside Car Park
Glenridding
Penrith
CA11 0PD
Tel: 017684 82414

Ambleside
Central Buildings
Market Cross
Ambleside
LA22 9BS
Tel: 015394 32582

Coniston
Ruskin Avenue
Coniston
LA21 8EH
Tel: 015394 41533

Other useful sources of information
Lake District Weatherline
Tel: 0844 846 2444
www.lakedistrictweatherline.co.uk

Mountain Weather Information Service
www.mwis.org.uk

Cumbria Tourism
www.golakes.co.uk

Traveline
Tel: 0871 200 2233
www.traveline.org.uk

Fix the Fells
www.fixthefells.co.uk

LISTING OF CICERONE GUIDES

The Southern Dales

SOUTHERN ENGLAND

20 Classic Sportive Rides in South East England
20 Classic Sportive Rides in South West England
Cycling in the Cotswolds
Mountain Biking on the North Downs
Mountain Biking on the South Downs
North Downs Way Map Booklet
South West Coast Path Map Booklet – Vol 1: Minehead to St Ives
South West Coast Path Map Booklet – Vol 2: St Ives to Plymouth
South West Coast Path Map Booklet – Vol 3: Plymouth to Poole
Suffolk Coast and Heath Walks
The Cotswold Way
The Cotswold Way Map Booklet
The Great Stones Way
The Kennet and Avon Canal
The Lea Valley Walk
The North Downs Way
The Peddars Way and Norfolk Coast path
The Pilgrims' Way
The Ridgeway Map Booklet
The Ridgeway National Trail
The South Downs Way
The South Downs Way Map Booklet
The South West Coast Path
The Thames Path
The Thames Path Map Booklet
The Two Moors Way
Two Moors Way Map Booklet
Walking Hampshire's Test Way
Walking in Cornwall
Walking in Essex
Walking in Kent
Walking in London
Walking in Norfolk
Walking in Sussex
Walking in the Chilterns
Walking in the Cotswolds
Walking in the Isles of Scilly
Walking in the New Forest
Walking in the North Wessex Downs
Walking in the Thames Valley
Walking on Dartmoor
Walking on Guernsey
Walking on Jersey
Walking on the Isle of Wight
Walking the Jurassic Coast
Walks in the South Downs National Park

BRITISH ISLES CHALLENGES, COLLECTIONS AND ACTIVITIES

The Big Rounds
The Book of the Bivvy
The Book of the Bothy

The C2C Cycle Route
The End to End Cycle Route
The End to End Trail
The Mountains of England and Wales: Vol 1 Wales
The Mountains of England and Wales: Vol 2 England
The National Trails
The UK's County Tops
Three Peaks, Ten Tors

ALPS CROSS-BORDER ROUTES

100 Hut Walks in the Alps
Across the Eastern Alps: E5
Alpine Ski Mountaineering Vol 1 – Western Alps
Alpine Ski Mountaineering Vol 2 – Central and Eastern Alps
Chamonix to Zermatt
The Karnischer Hohenweg
The Tour of the Bernina
Tour of Mont Blanc
Tour of Monte Rosa
Tour of the Matterhorn
Trail Running – Chamonix and the Mont Blanc region
Trekking in the Alps
Trekking in the Silvretta and Ratikon Alps
Trekking Munich to Venice
Walking in the Alps

PYRENEES AND FRANCE/SPAIN CROSS-BORDER ROUTES

Shorter Treks in the Pyrenees
The GR10 Trail
The GR11 Trail
The Pyrenean Haute Route
The Pyrenees
Walks and Climbs in the Pyrenees

AUSTRIA

Innsbruck Mountain Adventures
The Adlerweg
Trekking in Austria's Hohe Tauern
Trekking in the Stubai Alps
Trekking in the Zillertal Alps
Walking in Austria

SWITZERLAND

Switzerland's Jura Crest Trail
The Swiss Alpine Pass Route – Via Alpina Route 1
The Swiss Alps
Tour of the Jungfrau Region
Walking in the Bernese Oberland
Walking in the Engadine – Switzerland
Walking in the Valais

FRANCE

Chamonix Mountain Adventures
Cycle Touring in France
Cycling London to Paris
Cycling the Canal de la Garonne
Cycling the Canal du Midi
Écrins National Park

Mont Blanc Walks
Mountain Adventures in the Maurienne
The GR20 Corsica
The GR5 Trail
The GR5 Trail – Vosges and Jura
The Grand Traverse of the Massif Central
The Loire Cycle Route
The Moselle Cycle Route
The River Rhone Cycle Route
The Robert Louis Stevenson Trail
The Way of St James – Le Puy to the Pyrenees
Tour of the Oisans: The GR54
Tour of the Queyras
Vanoise Ski Touring
Via Ferratas of the French Alps
Walking in Corsica
Walking in Provence – East
Walking in Provence – West
Walking in the Auvergne
Walking in the Briançonnais
Walking in the Cevennes
Walking in the Dordogne
Walking in the Haute Savoie: North
Walking in the Haute Savoie: South
Walks in the Cathar Region

GERMANY

Hiking and Cycling in the Black Forest
The Danube Cycleway Vol 1
The Rhine Cycle Route
The Westweg
Walking in the Bavarian Alps

ICELAND AND GREENLAND

Trekking in Greenland – The Arctic Circle Trail
Walking and Trekking in Iceland

IRELAND

The Wild Atlantic Way and Western Ireland

ITALY

Italy's Sibillini National Park
Shorter Walks in the Dolomites
Ski Touring and Snowshoeing in the Dolomites
The Way of St Francis
Through the Italian Alps
Trekking in the Apennines
Trekking in the Dolomites
Via Ferratas of the Italian Dolomites Vol 1
Via Ferratas of the Italian Dolomites: Vol 2
Walking and Trekking in the Gran Paradiso
Walking in Abruzzo
Walking in Italy's Cinque Terre
Walking in Italy's Stelvio National Park
Walking in Sardinia
Walking in Sicily

For full information on all our
guides, books and eBooks,
visit our website:
www.cicerone.co.uk

Explore the world with Cicerone

walking • trekking • mountaineering • climbing • mountain biking • cycling • via ferratas • scrambling • trail running • skills and techniques

For over 50 years, Cicerone have built up an outstanding collection of nearly 400 guides, inspiring all sorts of amazing experiences.

www.cicerone.co.uk – where adventures begin

- Our **website** is a treasure-trove for every outdoor adventurer. You can buy books or read inspiring articles and trip reports, get technical advice, check for updates, and view videos, photographs and mapping for routes and treks.

- **Register this book** or any other Cicerone guide in your member's library on our website and you can choose to automatically access updates and GPX files for your books, if available.

- Our **fortnightly newsletters** will update you on new publications and articles and keep you informed of other news and events. You can also follow us on Facebook, Twitter and Instagram.

We hope you have enjoyed using this guidebook. If you have any comments you would like to share, please contact us using the form on our website or via email, so that we can provide the best experience for future customers.

CICERONE

Juniper House, Murley Moss Business Village, Oxenholme Road, Kendal LA9 7RL

✉ info@cicerone.co.uk   cicerone.co.uk

About the Author

Gillian Price was born in England but moved to Australia when young. After taking a degree in anthropology and working in adult education, she set off to travel through Asia and trek the Himalayas. The culmination of her journey was Venice where, her enthusiasm fired for mountains, the next logical step was towards the Dolomites, only hours away. Starting there, Gillian is steadily exploring the mountain ranges and flatter bits of Italy and bringing them to life for visitors in a series of outstanding guides for Cicerone.

When not out walking with Nicola, her Venetian cartographer husband, Gillian works as a freelance travel writer (www.gillianprice.eu). A strong promoter of public transport to minimise impact in alpine areas, she is an active member of the Italian Alpine Club CAI and Mountain Wilderness.

Other Cicerone guides by the author

Across the Eastern Alps – the E5
Gran Paradiso: Alta Via 2 Trek
   and Day Walks
Shorter Walks in the Dolomites
Through the Italian Alps – the GTA
Trekking in the Alps
   (contributing author)
Trekking in the Apennines –
   the GEA
Trekking in the Dolomites
Walking in Italy's Stelvio
   National Park

Walking in Sicily
Walking in the Central Italian Alps
Walking in the Dolomites
Walking in Tuscany
Walking on Corsica
Walking on the Amalfi Coast
Walking the Italian Lakes
Walks and Treks in the
   Maritime Alps